THE
EUGENIA FULLER ATWOOD
LIBRARY

BEAVER COLLEGE, GLENSIDE, PENNSYLVANIA

Gift of

WELSH POEMS

Sixth Century to 1600

edited by Gwyn Williams

PRESENTING WELSH POETRY

✻

by Gwyn Williams

TURKEY
EASTERN TURKEY

WELSH POEMS

Sixth Century to 1600

Translated with an introduction
and notes by
GWYN WILLIAMS

FABER AND FABER
3 Queen Square
London

First published in this edition 1973
by Faber and Faber Limited
3 Queen Square London WC1
Printed in Great Britain
by Whitstable Litho, Straker Brothers Ltd
All rights reserved

ISBN 0 571 10379 0

Published with the support of
the Welsh Arts Council

For

Teleri, Lowri and Gwydion

. . . A tall tree on the river's bank, one half of it burning from root to top, the other half in green leaf.

PEREDUR SON OF EFRAWG

Acknowledgements

I owe a debt of thanks to the following:
the Welsh scholars of this century who have transcribed and edited many of the old texts;

the National Library of Wales for so helpfully and efficiently putting before me the manuscripts and books I needed to consult;

Mr. John Lehmann, who published my translations of Dafydd ap Gwilym's *The Woodland Mass* and Iolo Goch's *The Labourer* in *The London Magazine*; Professor Idris Foster, who helped me towards an understanding of the early medieval poetry;

the Welsh Arts Council, for their assistance and advice;

and Dr. Thomas Parry, for the very valuable corrections and suggestions he offered in checking the translations for this present reprinting.

Any faults that remain in these translations are solely my own.

Contents

Acknowledgements 6

Introduction 9

Aneirin   1. Selections from 'The Gododdin' 17

Taliesin   2. The Battle of Argoed Llwyfain 20

Anonymous   3. Eagle of Pengwern 21

4. The Body of Urien Rheged 22

5. The Sick Man of Abercuawg 23

6. Stanzas of the Graves 25

7. Gereint Son of Erbin 27

Meilyr   8. Deathbed Poem 29

Cynddelw   9. Epigram 31

Gwalchmai   10. Exultation 32

Hywel ab Owain Gwynedd   11. Exultation 36

12. Ode I 39

13. Ode II 40

14. Ode III 41

15. Ode IV 42

16. Ode V 43

17. Ode VI 44

18. Ode VII 45

Gruffudd ab yr Ynad Coch

19. The Death of Llywelyn ap Gruffudd 46

Gruffudd ab Adda   20. Thief of Love 49

Dafydd ap Gwilym   21. The Woodland Mass 50

22. The Girls of Llanbadarn 52

23. The Rattle Bag 54

Llywelyn Goch   24. The Death of Lleucu Llwyd 56

Iolo Goch   25. The Labourer 50

26. Sir Hywel of the Axe 62

Siôn Cent   27. The Illusion of the World 65

7

Dafydd ab Edmwnd	28. To a Girl	68
	29. To a Girl's Hair	70
	30. Naming the Girl	72
	31. The Death of Siôn Eos	74
Bedo Aeddren	32. From Lent to Summer	76
Lewis Glyn Cothi	33. On the Death of his Son	78
Tudur Aled	34. To ask for a Stallion	80
Anonymous	35. To a Sweet-mouthed Girl	83
	36. Longing	84
	37. Three Hinds of Denbighshire	85
William Thomas	38. To the Harp	86
Robin Clidro	40. Marchan Wood	87
Anonymous	40. Glyn Cynon Wood	89
	41. Troelus and Cresyd (Act I sc. ii)	91
William Cynwal	42. The Defence of Woman	96
Thomas Prys	43. Trouble at Sea	105
	44. A Pretty Girl	108
	45. The Porpoise	109
Edmwnd Prys	46. A Welsh Ballad	112
Anonymous	47. The Lover's Shirt	115
	Notes	116
	Abbreviations	125
Index		126

Introduction

In the form in which it was first published, a form in which the original Welsh texts faced my translations, this book was entitled *The Burning Tree*[1] to suggest an outstanding mood of the Welsh poet, the awareness at the same time of contrary seasons and passions, a mood in which the poet brings into one phrase the force of love and war, of summer and winter, of holy sacrament and adulterous love.

Matthew Arnold in his *Study of Celtic Literature* notes a passage from the *Mabinogion* as an instance of what he calls Celtic magic. 'And they saw a tall tree by the side of the river, one half of which was in flames from the root to the top, and the other half was green and in full leaf.' It was enough for Arnold to recognize this as magic, distinguishing it from the radiant, uncomplicated Greek way of handling nature, without prying into the mechanics of the image. Coleridge might have helped him here, for this Celtic tree is a hitherto unapprehended relation of things, an integration of spring and autumn such as Spenser expressed in a more English way and at greater length in the stanza beginning:

> There is continuall Spring, and harvest there
> Continuall, both meeting at one tyme . . .
>
> (*Faerie Queene* III. xlii)

A similarly startling juxtaposition of the unexpected occurs in Keats's phrase 'fairy lands forlorn', which Arnold also quotes and in which he finds the very same note struck. That 'fairy lands forlorn' gives us one of the best examples in English of *cynghanedd* is accidental here. It is the suddenness and success of this linking of the previously held to be incongruous that makes metaphysical poetry and distinguishes Dafydd ap Gwilym from Chaucer, John Donne from Ben Jonson, Dylan Thomas from W. H. Auden. Out of such a vision too sprang the Old English poem *Seafarer*, which comes closest of all English poems to the mood of old Welsh writing, in which the cuckoo's note is a gloomy warning, as it is in old Welsh poetry, and the beauty of early summer is involved in the danger of death. Up to the end of the thirteenth century in Wales violence could and did alternate normally and closely with love-making,

[1] Faber and Faber, 1956

9

might be inseparably linked with it, and the return of the raiding season of the year made May as much a month of battle and sad remembering as of promise and joy.

Even in the earliest heroic verse this opposition is always to be found, though there is little talk of love. There the contrast is between the happy mead-drinking of the heroes in the prince's hall and the grim death in battle which was being prepared for, the vigorous youth of the warriors and the likelihood of their early killing, an opposition which is summed up in the phrase, 'he paid for his mead.' This payment for mead is in a Northern European tradition, for when in the Old English *Finn Fragment* the men of Hnaef's retinue fight to the last man, they too have paid for their mead. Of another hero of Mynyddawg Mwynfawr's retinue the contrast is made between his shyness and his courage,

> Diffun o flaen bun, medd a dalai.
> Breathless before a girl, he paid for his mead.

So too the whiteness of the skin of the dead warrior goes with the blackness of the raven which perches on his fallen body.

The young men of the *Gododdin*, drinking mead and wine from fine horns and gold, are drinking poison, according to the poet, who was one of their number, for in return for this hospitality they will go to battle and they will probably die. Vigour and death are thus in a normal association, and only the Sick Man of Abercuawg is safe in his deserted hut. The poets themselves often fought before composing accounts of battle and old Welsh law accorded a special reward to the poet who took part in the raid he celebrated. Aneirin may well have been the sole survivor of the commando raid on Catterick, and Taliesin and Myrddin, for I feel sure Myrddin must have existed, were warriors as well as poets. The twelfth-century professional poets Gwalchmai and Cynddelw boast of their reputation as warriors and could hardly have got away in their own time with a bogus claim. The warlike princes Owain Cyfeiliog and Hywel ab Owain Gwynedd were thoroughly trained in the art of versification, and it is Hywel ab Owain, son of the King of Gwynedd, who best achieved this fragmentation of impulses, this equivalent interlacing of the themes of love, landscape, war and death.

The absence of a centred design, of an architectural quality, is not a weakness in old Welsh poetry, but results quite reasonably from a specific view of composition. English and most Western European creative activity has been conditioned by the inheritance from Greece and Rome of the notion of a central point of interest in a poem, a picture or a play, a nodal region to which everything leads and upon which everything depends. The dispersed nature of the thematic splintering of Welsh poetry is not due to a failure to follow this classical convention. Aneirin, Gwalchmai, Cynddelw and Hywel ab Owain were not trying to write poems that would read like Greek temples or even Gothic cathedrals but, rather, like stone circles or the contour-following rings of the forts from which they fought, with hidden ways slipping from one ring to another. More obviously, their writing was like the inter-woven inventions preserved in early Celtic manuscripts and on stone crosses, where what happens in a corner is as important as what happens at the centre, because there often is no centre. That this idea of composition is still potent is demonstrated by the work of two great creative artists of Welsh blood of this present century, David Jones and Dylan Thomas. Of these two, David Jones is the more aware of the antiquity of the tradition in which he creates. *In Parenthesis* and *The Anathemata* are constructed on an inter-weaving pattern much like that of the *Gododdin* or Gwalchmai's *Gorhoffedd*, and one has only to contrast Jones's *Merlin Land*, or almost any other picture of his, with a Bellini or a Picasso to see how the thing works out in painting, how a dimension is created which is unachievable within the classical convention.

Sometimes, as in Meilyr's poem before his death and Gruffudd ab yr Ynad Coch's lament for the last ruler of independent Wales, there is only one theme and one mood is sustained throughout. Here we come closer to the development and climax to which we are accustomed in Western European art forms, but even here there is no logical sequence and the only art upon which one can draw for descriptive analogy, a process of dubious worth, is music of the complex sort. It must be remembered that all this early poetry was written, like music, to be listened to, not read. The hearer could not hold up the poem, as we sometimes do in reading, for the eye to go back over an earlier line. Echoing, running parenthesis, the purposeful re-iteration which has been given the ugly name of incremental repetition, the identity of end and beginning, all these are devices by which the poet attempts a collateral rather than a consecutive presentation of his experience, creating a dimension which thus cheats time, during the space of our listening to his poem. This is the trick which Dylan Thomas brings off in his *Prologue* to the *Collected Poems*, with its returning rhyme scheme, as does James Joyce in his prose experiments. The cuckoo's call echoes through the Abercuawg stanzas, the slim white corpse of Urien Rheged is brought again and again to the mind's eye in the lament for his death, and in *Gereint Filius Erbin* the horses recur with slight differences till one's mind is full of their colour and speed and the blood in which they have trampled and the thunder of their attack, which is like fire on a mountain, until suddenly comes the astonishing line *Pan aned Gereint oedd agored pyrth Nef*, and the simple vowels and simple diction make everything open and clear and calm. You cannot say that *Gereint Filius Erbin* has form or development in the accepted sense and yet it is the assured work of a master in words.

By the fourteenth century raiding and warfare are no longer part of the regular experience or subject matter of the poet. There is still an outlet for the determinedly pugnacious spirit and Iolo Goch's Sir Hywel of the Axe performs prodigies in France on behalf of the English king. But Gruffudd ab Adda's night raid is now not for cattle but for a girl. Dafydd ap Gwilym goes to church to look at the girls and turns his back to the altared God to stare over his plumed hat at the village beauties. The beauty of the world and the glory of God are brought into equally startling juxtaposition when Dafydd hears Mass sung by those traditional birds of love and summer, the thrush and the nightingale.

Aubade and serenade had come into Welsh from Provençal, perhaps through Dafydd ap Gwilym's Norman-French acquaintances at Newcastle Emlyn, but an aubade to a dead girl was something new, and Llywelyn Goch's macabre knocking at the earth-door of his dead Lleucu Llwyd set a new fashion in laments for a dead love. Here again there is a terrible opposition in the irony that runs through the poem.

For Siôn Cent the magic and colour of this world is all illusion and he is the first to take the flattering glove off the egalitarian hand of death in speaking to the great ones of this world, though Iolo Goch in his ploughman poem had already shown the virtue of the simple way of life at a time when the first seeds of democracy were being sown. But Bedo Aeddren, Dafydd Nanmor, Dafydd ab Edmwnd, Tudur Aled, Thomas Prys and a host of others continue to take an unequivocal delight in the loveliness of this world's things and experiences. The keening in Lewis Glyn Cothi's lament for his dead son is touched with the innocence and simplicity of its occasion.

There is not much that is political in the poems selected and translated for this volume. The early heroic work naturally shows a clean detestation of the enemy. From the ninth to the fifteenth century a considerable body of vaticinatory verse was produced as propaganda and encouragement for leaders and their factions in internecine and anti-English wars. Both sides in the Wars of the Roses had their poets in Wales and the prophecies concerning Henry Tudor at least were fulfilled even though the more numerous ones written for his uncle, Jasper Tudor, fell flat. But Henry's conquest of England did not turn out quite as his Welsh supporters had hoped. The absence of political opinion in the work of Dafydd ap Gwilym is significant, for after the loss of Welsh independence the religion of the woods held a positive protest as well as an escape, and Dafydd's feelings are made clear only by the contempt with which he uses the word English. Iolo Goch, chief praiser of Owain Glyndŵr, died before Glyndwr's war against England and he had accepted the situation to the degree of writing a poem in praise of Edward III. We learn what Dafydd ab Edmwnd thought of England and its laws from his poem on the death of Siôn Eos, John Nightingale the harpist, and he regrets that the more reasonable laws of Hywel Dda are no longer valid. In the sixteenth century strong feelings were aroused by the cutting down of Welsh woods for charcoal-burning, feelings similar to those evoked to-day by the afforestation or the depopulation for different purposes of Welsh hill country. Lively poems like *Coed Marchan* and *Coed Glyn Cynon* record protests against Elizabethan deforestation.

One of the subtlest pieces of political analysis in Welsh is the first scene of the tragedy of *Troelus a Chresyd*, which was probably written between 1600 and 1610. Like the scene included in this book it has no known source in any other version of this story and, unlike all other versions, it gives us Calchas' reasons for his defection to the Greeks. Apart from Shakespeare's *Coriolanus*, there is no better study in literature of the mind of the Quisling, and there were undoubtedly Welshmen in Elizabethan England who might appear in this light, perhaps even the great Cecil himself. But *Troelus a Chresyd* stands outside the poor, thin, broken tradition of Welsh drama. Its author, so far unidentified, was a scholar familiar with the London theatre and with English literature. A true Renaissance man, like Wyatt, Surrey and Spenser, his purpose was to fill a conspicuous gap in the literature of his country. Hugh Holland is the most likely author, but there is no direct evidence yet to tie him to the play.

Like *Troelus a Chresyd*, William Cynwal's *Defence of Woman* is in a European tradition, that of satirical sex-antagonism, of the *Schole House of Women*, the *Araith Ddychan i'r Gwragedd* and *Les Quinze Joyes de Mariage*, a battle which in France was carried on into the eighteenth century by Perrault, Boileau and Régnard.

Thomas Prys of Plas Iolyn spent years away from Wales, on sea, on the Continent and in Elizabethan London, getting to know its great houses, taverns, brothels and gaols from the inside, as his verse makes clear, without sacrificing any of his Welshness. From English example he may have borrowed the urge to tell a story in verse, a rare thing in a language where prose had always been the medium of continuous narrative. And in his *cywydd To a Pretty Girl* he reflects the London fashion in this matter by abandoning the stock Welsh comparisons for beauty, Indeg, Tegau and Gwenhwyfar, for the classical Venus, Lucrece, Helen, Cressida and Diana.

But it was Prys's outspoken independence of mind and his know-
ledge and love of the sea that brought in the elements most likely
to refresh the stiffening conventions of verse in the strict metres.
In all the poems of asking, no one had before asked for and des-
cribed a Spanish boat, nor had the splendid porpoise before appeared
amongst the likely and unlikely creatures called upon by the poets
to carry their messages of love and friendship. This is what Sheridan
might have called the messenger referential, for no more suitable
envoy than a porpoise can be thought of to carry a message to a
sailor. Dafydd ap Gwilym was inconsiderate enough to ask a wood-
cock to be his love-messenger to a girl. Thomas Prys employs a flea
for this purpose and surely no creature can get nearer or more
secretly to a girl than a flea. There is freshness, boldness and artistry
in the work of Thomas Prys.

With the decline of poetry in the strict metres, the end of the
sixteenth century saw experiments in the free measures, stanza
forms outside the classical twenty-four metres of the highest class
of bardic production, and a prosody which did not require the
formal use of *cynghanedd*. The new forms were sometimes based on
English songs, but more often on old Welsh forms like the *awdl-
gywydd* couplet, such forms as had been used for centuries by the
lesser, more popular orders of poets in Wales in poems which were
not thought worthy of recording, and which have therefore been
lost to us, except for the scraps preserved in the folk memory and
known as *hen benillion* (old stanzas) or *penillion telyn* (stanzas for
the harp).

This book begins with a company of young men going south-
wards to Catterick to their death in a late sixth-century battle, and
ends with a girl washing her lover's shirt under Cardigan Bridge,
and a thread of gold runs through from beginning to end, from the
gold-embroidered tunics of the British warriors to the golden wash-
beetle the girls tells us she uses to drub the dirt. But a thousand
years of continuous and copious versification cannot be fully repre-
sented in one volume and there are important aspects of Welsh
poetry which are not exemplified here. The poem of political pro-
phecy, the poem in praise of God, the nonsense poem, the rabelaisian

satire, gnomic verse, the disputation, the *awdl* to the noble patron, the poem of genealogy, there would be no end to the additions and the book would become unmanageable. I have gathered together and attempted to translate poems[1] which I enjoy reading, a good many modes are covered and the three main themes of love, death and the beauty of this world are always present.

The millennium from the year 600 to 1600 saw the development and decline of poetry in the strict Welsh metres and the perfection and classification of the sound-echoing devices known as *cynghanedd*. Technically the peak came with Dafydd ab Edmwnd in the middle of the fifteenth century. The twenty-four measures, already classified in the fourteenth century, were by him tightened up and made more difficult in order to discourage the half-trained practitioner in verse. But a high degree of metrical and phonetic skill is to be observed in the very earliest Welsh verse and one remembers Julius Caesar's statement that the Druids used verse as a pedagogical device. According to pre-Christian Greek travellers to Britain, the word *bardd*, still the Welsh word for a poet, was in use at the beginning of the first century B.C. And when I refer to the decline of poetry in the strict metres with the outburst of verse in the new stanza forms at the end of the sixteenth century, let it not be thought that the twenty-four measures[2] have since fallen into desuetude or become merely museum pieces. They have been in continuous use, and a knowledge of them is essential to anyone who hopes to win the chair at the National Eisteddfod. And at least two of the old measures, the *englyn* and the *cywydd*, are in regular use by a very large number of writers to-day.

[1] A few are complete versions of poems partially translated for my *Introduction to Welsh Poetry* (Faber & Faber, 1953), a critical and historical account of the period covered by the translations of this present book.

[2] For a full treatment, in Welsh, of Welsh prosody, see *Cerdd Dafod,* Sir John Morris Jones (Oxford University Press). A summary of the twenty-four metres and of the rules of *cynghanedd*, in English, appears in an appendix to my *Introduction to Welsh Poetry.*

1. The Gododdin (Selected stanzas)

The men who went to Catraeth were a speedy band,
fresh mead their sustenance, it became bitterness.
Three hundred were in order embattled,
and after rejoicing there came silence.
Though they went to churches to do penance
death, the tale is true, got them. (ll. 68–74)

The men who went to Catraeth at dawn
had their lives cut short by their spirit.
They drank the sweet snare of yellow mead
and many a musician was gay for a year.
Red their swords; never cleanse their spear-blades;
shields were white, spear-heads four-edged
before Mynyddog Mwynfawr's band. (90–96)

The men who went to Catraeth were famous,
wine and mead from gold was their drink
for a year according to honoured custom,
three hundred and sixty-three gold-collared men.
Of those who attacked after flowing drink
only three escaped from the fury of battle,
Aeron's two wardogs and Cynon steel-hard,
and I from my bleeding for my song's sake. (235–242)

It was true, as Catlew said,
that no one's horses could catch Marchlew.
He hurled spears in battle
from a broad-tracked, leaping horse,
though not bred for burdens at the gate.
His sword-stroke was bold at his post;
he flung ash spears from the square
of his fist, from the back of a slim, steaming horse.
This very dear one shared his copious wine;
he killed with furious, blood-flecked sword.

As harvesters reap in changing weather
so Marchlew caused the blood to flow. (300–311)

Issac of the South land was outstanding,
his ceremonies were like the flowing sea,
    gaiety, free-handedness,
    fine mead-drinking.
    Where he dug in his weapon
    he sought no more revenge.
When fierce he was fierce, there was no change of mood,
his sword rang in the heads of mothers;
a wall in battle, Gwyddneu's son is praised. (318–326)

Ceredig, the loved leader
and passionate champion in war,
the gold-patterned shield of battle:
spears were splintered and broken,
like a grown man he held his place with the spears;
before being pressed down by earth, before agony,
with his weapons he held his place in the rank.
May he be welcomed in Heaven's company
by the Trinity in perfect union.

When Caradawg rushed to battle
like a wild boar, a killer of three chiefs,
the bull of the band, a cutter-down in fighting,
he fed the wolves with his hand.
This is my witness, that Owain ap Eulad
and Gwrien and Gwyn and Gwriad,
from Catraeth, from the killing,
from Hyddwn Hill before it was taken,
after having shining mead in their hands
not one ever saw his father again.

The men who attacked leapt forward together,
in their brief lives were drunk on distilled mead;
Mynyddawg's army, famed in battle,
their lives paid for their feast of mead.
Caradawg and Madawg, Pyll and Ieuan,

Gwgawn and Gwiawn, Gwyn and Cynvan,
Peredur of steel weapons, Gwawrddur and Aeddan,
attackers in battle, they had their shields broken;
and though they were killed, they killed.
Not one came back to his belongings. (333–362)

Men went to Catraeth in a band, with a shout,
with the power of horses and trappings and shields,
with shafts held ready and pointed spears,
with gleaming armour and with swords.
He led, he cut through armies,
five fifties fell before his blades:
Rhufawn Hir gave gold to the altar
and a reward and a fair gift to the singer. (372–379)

These warriors set out and met together,
and all of one mind they attacked.
Short their lives, long the yearning for them by their
    kinsmen.
They killed seven times their number of English;
in battle they made widowed women
and many a mother with tears on her eyelids. (668–673).

From wine and mead-drinking they went from us,
these armed ones: I know death's sad tale.
Before these grew grey their killing happened.
Towards Catreath their band was speedy,
but of Mynyddawg's retinue (o grief!)
of the three hundred one only returned. (689–694)

2. *The Battle of Argoed Llwyfain*

On Saturday morning there was a great battle
from the rising of the sun until it set.
Fflamddwyn's men set out in four bands;
Goddau and Rheged formed their ranks
in Dyfwy, from Argoed to Arfynydd.
They were not allowed to delay for one day.
Out called Fflamddwyn, the great noise-maker,
'Have my hostages come? Are they ready?'
Owain, wounder of the east, answered,
'Neither come, nor here, nor are they ready.'
A whelp of Coel's line would be hard put to it
before he gave anyone as a hostage.
Then Urien shouted, the lord of Yrechwydd,
'If there's to be gathering to talk of peace,
let us raise our rampart on the mountain
and raise our faces above the shield's edge.
Let us raise spears above men's heads
and fall on Fflamddwyn amongst his hosts
and kill both him and his company!'

   In front of Argoed Llwyfain
   many a corpse was made;
the crows grew red from the warriors.
The army attacked, with their chieftain.
For a year I'll sing the song of their victory.
When I'm old and decline to death's stubborn need
I'll not be content unless praising Urien.

3. Eagle of Pengwern

Eagle of Pengwern, grey-crested, tonight
    its shriek is high,
    eager for flesh I loved.

Eagle of Pengwern, grey-crested, tonight
    its call is high,
    eager for Cynddylan's flesh.

Eagle of Pengwern, grey-crested, tonight
    its claw is high,
    eager for flesh I love.

Eagle of Pengwern, it called far tonight,
    it kept watch on men's blood;
    Trenn shall be called a luckless town.

Eagle of Pengwern, it calls far tonight,
    it feasts on men's blood;
    Trenn shall be called a shining town.

4. *The Body of Urien Rheged*

The slim white corpse that is buried to-day
    under earth and stones:
  woe to my hand that Owain's father is killed.

The slim white corpse that is buried to-day
    between earth and oak:
  woe to me that my cousin is killed.

The slim white corpse that is buried to-day
    and left under stones:
  woe to my hand the lot that was doomed to me.

The slim white corpse that is buried to-day
    in earth and turf:
  woe to my hand that Cynfarch's son was killed.

The slim white corpse that is buried to-day
    under gravel and a mark:
  woe to my hand the lot that has befallen me.

The slim white corpse that is buried to-day
    under earth and grit:
  woe to my hand the lot that was thrown to me.

The slim white corpse that is buried to-day
    under earth and nettles:
  woe to my hand the lot that was caused me.

The slim white corpse that is buried to-day
    under earth and blue stones:
  woe to my hand the lot that caught me.

5. The Sick Man of Aber Cuawg

To sit high on a hill is the wish of my heart,
    yet it does not rouse me:
  my journey's short, my little homestead's empty.

The breeze is sharp, cowherds are ragged:
    whilst trees put on the fair colour
  of summer, I am very sick to-day.

I'm not light-footed, I keep no retinue,
    I can't go visiting:
  whilst it pleases the cuckoo, let it sing.

The clamorous cuckoo sings at dawn
    a high song over Cuawg's meadows:
  better a spendthrift than a miser.

At Aber Cuawg cuckoos sing
    on flowering branches:
  clamorous cuckoo, may it sing on.

At Aber Cuawg cuckoos sing
    on flowering branches:
  wretched sick man who hears them all the time!

At Aber Cuawg cuckoos sing:
    bitter it is to my mind
  that one who once heard them hears them no more.

I listened to the cuckoo in the ivy tree:
    my garment is slack,
  my longing is greater for those I loved.

High up above the splendid oak
  I heard the voice of birds:
  o loud cuckoo, we remember those we love!

Singer of constant song, with longing in its cry,
  wanderer, with the speed of a hawk,
  the cuckoo calls at Aber Cuawg.

6. Stanzas of the Graves

The graves that a shower wets,
of men not slain stealthily,
Gwên and Urien and Uriad.

At Aber Gwenoli is Pryderi's grave
where the waves pound the land;
Gwallawg Hir's grave is at Carrawg.

In the earth's far corner is Owain ap Urien's grave:
under the gravel of Morfael's ground
at Abererch is Rhydderch Hael.

Whose is this grave? One of good name
who made ordered battle against the English;
this is the grave of Gwên ap Llywarch Hen.

Three graves of three steadfast ones on an outstanding hill
in the fair valley of Gwynionawg—
Mor and Meilir and Madawg.

Hidden far from the turmoil,
the mould of Machavwy hides them,
the long white fingers of red Beidog.

Whose is this grave on the hill's side?
Many who do not know ask:
a grave for Coel, son of Cynfelyn.

Whose is the four-square grave
with the four stones about its head?
The grave of Madawg, savage horseman.

Proud Siawn's grave in the mountain's long acre,
between gravel and oak;
he laughed in bitter, treacherous times.

There are few to lament the graves on the strand;
here is Sanawg, proud girl, here's Rhun, battle-seeker,
here's Carrwen, daughter of Hennin, here are Lledin and Llywy.

Whose is the grave in the great plain?
His hand was proud upon his blades:
the grave of Beli, giant Benlli's son.

7. Gereint Son of Erbin

Before Gereint, the enemy's punisher,
I saw white stallions with red shins
and after the war-cry a bitter grave.

Before Gereint, the enemy's depriver,
I saw stallions red-shinned from battle
and after the war-cry a bitter pensiveness.

Before Gereint, scourge of the enemy,
I saw stallions girdled in white
and after the war-cry a bitter covering.

At Llongborth I saw vultures
and more than many a bier
and men red before Gereint's onrush.

At Llongborth I saw slaughter,
men in fear and blood on the head
before Gereint, his father's great son.

At Llongborth I saw spurs
and men who would not flinch from spears
and the drinking of wine from shining glass.

At Llongborth I saw armour
and the blood flowing
and after the war-cry a bitter burying.

At Llongborth I saw Arthur,
where brave men struck down with steel,
an emperor, a director of toil.

At Llongborth Gereint was killed,
and brave men from Devon's lowland;
and before they were killed, they killed.

There were fast horses under Gereint's thigh,
long-shanked, wheat-fed;
they were red, in their rush like milky eagles.

There were fast horses under Gereint's thigh,
long-shanked, grain nourished them;
they were red, their rush like black eagles.

There were fast horses under Gereint's thigh,
long-shanked, devourers of grain;
they were red, their rush like red eagles.

There were fast horses under Gereint's thigh,
long-shanked, emptiers of grain;
they were red, their rush like white eagles.

There were fast horses under Gereint's thigh,
long-shanked, with the stride of a stag,
like the roar of burning on a waste mountain.

There were fast horses under Gereint's thigh,
long-shanked, greedy for grain,
blue-gray, their hair tipped with silver.

There were fast horses under Gereint's thigh,
long-shanked, worthy of grain;
they were red, their rush like grey eagles.

There were fast horses under Gereint's thigh,
long-shanked, grain-fed;
they were red, their rush like brown eagles.

When Gereint was born, Heaven's gates were open,
Christ would grant what was asked:
a fair countenance, the glory of Britain.

8. Deathbed Poem

Rex regum, whom it's easy to praise,
I offer a prayer to my Lord above,
the ruling lord of the heavenly circle:
o Good One, make a pact with me!
Frail and vain is my memory of having
angered you; and I am repentant.
I have committed sin in God's presence,
I have not observed my true religion.
Yet must I needs serve my Lord God
before I'm weakly put in earth.
A true prophecy to Adam and his breed
did the prophets declare,
the abode of Jesus in Mary Virgin,
and the happy Mary bore the child.
I gathered a burden of wild sins
and I was frightened in their tumult.
Lord of all places, how good you are to praise!
I will praise you, that I may cleanse myself before being punished.
The King of all lords who knows me, won't deny me
his mercy for my wickedness.
I was given plentiful gold and silk
by generous lords for praising them,
but after the lively gift of verse
my wretched tongue is struck with silence.
May I, the poet Meilyr, pilgrim to Peter,
gatekeeper who judges the sum of virtues,
when the time comes for us to arise
who are in the grave, have thy support.
May I be at home awaiting the call
in a fold with the moving sea near it,
a hermitage of perpetual honour
with a bosom of brine about its graves.

Island of fair Mary, pure island of the pure,
how lovely to await resurrection there!
Christ of the foretold cross knows and will keep me
from pain of hell, that guest-house apart.
The Creator who created me will take me in
to the good parish of Enlli's people.

9. *Epigram*

Sung by Cynddelw to the huntsmen of Llywelyn son of Madoc, son of Maredudd, and to his horns, for their gift to him of the stag they killed near his house.

Proud its call when its cry is raised,
when horns are blown in concord,
horn of Llywelyn, lord of great hosts,
broad-based, thin-mouthed and loud of blast.

A horn after killing, a happy horn,
horn of Llywelyn's advance guard,
a horn of wood, a brave man sounds it,
a tapering horn in the track of hounds.

10. *Exultation*

Early rises the sun, summer hastens on,
splendid the speech of birds, fine smooth weather;
I am of noble habits, fearless in battle,
I am a lion, my onrush a flash before a host.
I watched all night to keep a border,
the bubbling waters of the fords of Dygen Freiddin,
the open grassland all green, the water shining,
loud the nightingale's familiar song,
gulls playing on the sea's surface,
their feathers glistening, their ranks turbulent.
My memory travels far in early summer,
because I love a young girl of Caerwys.
You are far from the lively folk of little Anglesey,
carefree under its covering secrecy.
I listened once on a true occasion
to the gentle words of a fawn of a girl.
Then to the advantage of generous Owain, my fine fetter,
the English retreat before my sword.

My sword flashes, a lightning to guard the brave,
there is shining gold on my buckler;
streams are impetuous, the day is warm,
birds are tuneful in song, their busy poetry.
My thoughts are proud and in a far place to-day,
going as far as Efyrnwy land.
White are the tips of the apple trees with clusters of flowers,
trees are proudly clad, every mind flies to its love.
I love a Caerwys girl of noble qualities
and hate those who won't stand by her.
Genilles sharpens me, though she kill me. By the word
of my lord, this visit's important to me.
Blessed is he to whom God grants
a bright girl's virgin favour, gentle beauty.

My sword flashes, its nature is lightning in battle;
there's shining gold on my shield.
Many of the girls of Gwent praise me
who have never seen me, they're eager to mention me.
I saw before Owain the Angles in their ruin
and near Rhibyll a lord in battle.
I am called Gwalchmai, foe to the Saxons,
at the call of Môn's lord I plunged into battle.
And to win favour of my pretty one, like snow on trees,
when they fought before the fort, I shed blood.

Bloody is my sword and fierce in battle;
in conflict with England a hero doesn't hide.
I saw from the onslaught of the warrior-son of Gruffudd
champions cut down, and a broken rout;
Owain's raging battle at Aber Teifi,
blessed king of Britain, possessing lord,
a chieftain collapses, hearing him there,
with the blood of battle before Iago's great grandson.
I am called Gwalchmai, foe to Edwin and the Angles,
in the tumult of the host I am a killer.
I have my witnesses who have my evidence
of the descendant of Cynan, of Coel's triumphant line;
and to please him on the proud hill's side of Breiddin,
I'll not avoid battle through any confusion.
I love May's nightingale which hinders morning sleep
and the slow looks of the white-cheeked girl.
I love fine, stag-like horses and well-fed,
the confining of sorrow and the harness of battle. . . .

My sword is a flash, it won't do to insult me;
I don't restrain my hand from killing, it's bitter.
I saw the violence of a king before Gwythyr's rock,
when he fought with Môn's sweet-tempered lord.
I saw Rhuddlan a surge of flame before Owain
and stiffened corpses and red spears.
I saw there a busy surrendering,
the silencing of a hundred chiefs through recklessness;
Carmarthen destroyed in a great onslaught,

loud-mouthed for prey the eagle of Emreis.
Let kings bring tribute to him,
lord of Aberffraw and Ynyr's land.
I listened to the nightingale and longed for the shy one,
the spear was deep-hued, my mind wandered far;
the girl is not asleep, I know how far.
When the apple bough end is a mound of bloom,
the wave is foam-topped at Porth Wygyr.
A chieftain is wise, loving and famous:
to dream of a girl proud-hued like frost-flakes
is splendid at night, or may I be spared it. . . .

The green wave by Aberffraw woke me,
it strikes at the land, it bears riches,
bravely the birds sing around it.
There's a pleasant wood with safety in it,
a secluded thicket house, a silent stronghold,
a home for me, easy, hospitable.
My horse is fiery on Caeo field
in the cause of Cynan's lord of glorious qualities,
the famous one of holy Gwynedd, say all,
key-bearer of Britain, owning everything.
I listened to an eagle at his dinner of meat,
Gwynedd came with blood for him.
When Owain seized the gold and the houses of Denbigh,
a day when shields were worn out in the field,
I pounced upon the English hosts.
There was grief in England before my hand's path,
my virtue merited my choosing
as descendant of Cadell in Tysilio's land.

The green wave at Aber Dau woke me,
it strikes at the grey shore with its fair streams,
bravely the birds sing there;
a place for my enemies to retreat from.
I know wild grass which confidently grows,
I know the proud tree-covering, its flowers are lovely.
I know that I drank mead served to me from gold
in the hall of tall Owain, brave worthy one.

His wine was poured to me from the lord's white hand,
in a fort in Arfon near Hiriell's land.
It was granted to my hand to kill by intent
at Maes Garnedd field in the company of lords.
He pours forth wealth and wealthy gifts;
he carries Britain's praise to earth's four corners,
he gets pledges from Dumbarton in the north,
he's a dragon in war and blessed in the south.

Early summer is pleasant, the weather fine,
the lovely, happy summer gently lingers;
the waters gently gather, the turf laughs by the running water
of Ogwen, Cegin and Clywedog streams.
The sea wave with its great roar woke me,
steadily flowing from Aber Menai;
the white waves pound under the Great Orme,
the seashore of Lord Maelgwn's maidens.
I went over the Lliw to the homesteads of Lothian,
to within sight of the golden fort of Arderydd.
And I was asked which of Britain's kings
is the most generous of feast-giving breasts,
and I declared it without shame
that he was Owain, for long much-pledged one of Christendom.
Deprived of a girl, the stuff of heaven's light,
who contracted with me a long friendship,
there came to me a new wasting,
with her long brown lashes and long soft cheek;
in a hall of plenty I'll be desired,
tonight I'll be easy if I'm given freedom;
and if God in heaven is on my side,
being with my bright girl will be my lulling.

11. *Exultation*

A foaming white wave washes over a grave,
the tomb of Rhufawn Pebyr, regal chieftain.
I love to-day what the English hate, the open land of the North,
and the varied growth that borders the Lliw.
I love those who gave me my fill of mead,
where the seas reach in long contention.
I love its household and its strong buildings
and at its lord's wish to go to war.
I love its strand and its mountains,
its castle near the woods and its fine lands,
its water meadows and its valleys,
its white gulls and its lovely women.
I love its soldiers, its trained stallions,
its woods, its brave men and its homes.
I love its fields under the little clover,
where honour was granted a secure joy.
I love its regions, to which valour entitles,
its wide waste lands and its wealth.
O, Son of God, how great a wonder,
how splendid the stags, great their possessions!
With the thrust of a spear I did splendid work
between the host of Powys and lovely Gwynedd.
On a pale white horse, a rash adventure,
may I now win freedom from my exile.
I'll never hold out till my people come;
a dream says so and God wills so.
A foaming white wave washes over a grave.

A white wave, near the homesteads, foams over,
coloured like hoar-frost in the hour of its advance.
I love the sea-coast of Meirionnydd,
where a white arm was my pillow.
I love the nightingale in the wild wood,
where two waters meet in that sweet valley.

Lord of heaven and earth, ruler of Gwynedd,
how far Kerry[1] is from Caer Lliwelydd!
In Maelienydd I mounted on a bay
and rode night and day to Rheged.
May I have, before my grave, a new conquest,
the land of Tegeingl, fairest in the world.
Though I be a lover of Ovid's way,
may God be mindful of me at my end.
A white wave, near the homesteads, foams over.

I salute the most high lord,
the most worthy one, because he's a king.
I compose a poem in the first place,
a song of praise like Merlin sang,
my skill in verse to the women who own it,
(how hesitant their virtue makes them!)
the best in all the country west
of Chester gates to Porth Ysgewin.

One is a girl who must be chiefly praised,
        Gwenllian, summer-weather-hued;
    the second is the one in the mantle and gold collar;
    my lips are far from her.

Fair Gweirfyl, my gift, my mystery, whom I never had;
        whom not one of my kin won;
    though I be killed with double-edged blades,
    it grieves me for the wife of a king's foster-brother.

For seemly Gwladus, shy, childish young woman,
        beloved of the people,
    I'll compose a secret sigh,
    I'll praise her with the yellow of the gorse.

Soon may I see, with my vigour far removed from his
        and with my sword in my hand,
    bright Lleucu, my love, laughing;
    her husband won't laugh before the onrush.

        [1] *V.* note on page 118 for these place names.

37

I am involved in the strife that has come to me
   and longing, alas, is natural,
 for pretty Nest, like apple blossom,
 my golden passion, heart of my sin.

For the virgin Generys who does not relieve my passion;
   may she not insist on chastity!
 For Hunydd there's matter till Doomsday,
 for Hawis my chosen ritual.

I had a girl of the same mind one day;
I had two, their praise be the greater;
I had three and four and fortune;
I had five, splendid in their white flesh;
I had six without concealing sin;
a bright girl from above the white fort came to me;
I had seven and an arduous business it was;
I had eight, repaying some of the praise I sang;
   teeth are good to keep the tongue quiet!

12. Ode I

I love summer time and the thronging of horses;
a war-band is eager before a brave lord.
The wave's topped with foam, there is swift saddling;
the apple-tree has put on another sign.
My shield is bright on my shoulder for battle;
I loved her who wasn't given to me, in spite of desire.
Slowly the tall white hemlock weakly leans,
coloured like bright dawn even at resting time,
shining, frail, fair, pensive, white and gentle.
In stepping over reeds she almost falls,
the pretty darling, weakly leaning.
She's not much older than a ten years old girl,
childish, shapely, full of seemliness.
Her childhood training was to give freely;
as a young woman more lust will fall on the girl
than unseemly words from her mouth.
Shall I, a walking suppliant, have a tryst?
How long must I beg you? Come out to meet me!
I have grown weak in the madness of love;
Jesus, who understands, won't reprove me.

13. Ode II

I love a fine-built fort in a crescent of hills,
where a proud form breaks into my sleep.
A notable, resolute man will get through to it,
the savage, vocal wave howls to it,
chosen place of a beauty whose qualities shine.
Bright and shining it rises from the ocean shore
to the woman who shines upon this year.
A year in Snowdonia, in desolate Arfon:
no one who deserves a pavilion or a silk mantle
do I love more than I love her.
If she granted her favour in return for my verse,
I would be next to her every night.

14. Ode III

I would beg to-day for a gleaming grey horse
and ride through to the fine land of Cynlas
to seek a talking time, before death takes me;
in sleep to check a liveliness that has hindered me.
My standard as a youth of honour
was her colour, like the blue-white waves.
My memory lingers in her company,
longing for her whilst she hates me.
Though I may do the girl honour by my praise,
suffering doesn't help me; what lineage satisfies?
This heart is broken, it has a yearning;
for the slim-growing girl red gold is no prop
to-day; my support is not enough,
where once was my relationship.
O, God's one Son, of heaven's kingdom,
before dwelling in this pain why wasn't I killed ?

15. Ode IV

My choice, a slim, fair, comely girl,
tall, lovely in her heather-coloured gown.
My chosen experience, to look at womanliness
when it quietly utters a seemly thought.
My choice is to share with and be with a girl
privately, with secrets and with gifts.
My choice, fair colour of the wave,
wise one in your country, is your elegant Welsh.
You are my choice. How do I stand with you?
Why are you silent, my pretty silence?
I've chosen a girl of whom I'll not repent:
it's right to choose a lovely girl of choice.

16. Ode V

I love a bright fort on a shining slope,
where a fair, shy girl loves watching gulls.
I'd like to go, though I get no great love,
on a longed-for visit on a slender white horse
to seek my love of the quiet laughter,
to recite love, since it's come my way,
to restore me from my gloom, and its half light,
to restore to me one skin-coloured like the wave.
A flowing from her domain had come to us,
colour of snow gleaming on a cold height.
Lest I be angered in Ogrfan's hall,
reluctant to leave her, a warrior's death,
she has taken my life away; I am made feeble.
In my desire I am like Garwy Hir
for a girl kept from me in Ogrfan's hall.

17. Ode VI

When crows were happy, when blood gushed,
    when blood spouted,
  when it was war, when its houses were reddened,
  when it was Rhuddlan, when the red hall flamed;

when the crimson red flame flamed to heaven
    and a house was no shelter;
  the bright burning of it was easily seen
  from the White Fort near Menai's shore.

On the third day of May, three hundred ships foundered
    of the fleet of the king's household,
  and a beardless warrior put to flight
  a thousand leaders on Menai water.

18. Ode VII

When the sky darkened above, when foreigners were taken,
    when the king was routed,
  when warriors were armed for battle,
  when there was a weapon struck at a beard;

in Gorwynwy woods punishing England
    and spoiling its homesteads;
  with a hand on the cross a host rushed forward.

There was killing, and a band with blood-sprinkled blades,
    and the colour of blood on a rabble;
  a bloody sheet over heads and leaders,
  a place of blood and blood-stained cheeks.

19. *The Death of Llywelyn ap Gruffudd*

The heart is cold under a breast of pitiful fear
    for a king, the oaken door of Aberffraw.
Fine gold was paid to us from his hand
and he deserved the golden chaplet.
Golden horns of a golden king do not bring me the joy
    of Llywelyn; I am not free to arm as I would.
Woe to me for my lord, the unshamed hawk,
    woe for the calamity of his bringing down.
Woe for the loss, woe for the destiny,
    woe for the news that he has a wound.
Cadwaladr of defence, protection's sharp piercer,
    he of the red spear, golden-handed ruler,
he shared out wealth, every winter he dressed me
    in the garments he had worn.
Lord of great herds, there's no more prospering,
but for him there remains eternal life.
My wrath's on the Englishman for despoiling me;
mine is the need to bewail his death.
I have cause to speak harshly with God
    who has left me without him.
Mine is it to praise without stint or stop,
mine is it from now on long to remember him.
All my life long my grief will be for him;
    since the grief is mine, mine is the weeping.
I've lost a lord and I grasp a long fear,
for a hand has killed the lord of the court.
O good true Lord, listen to me,
how loud I bewail; woe to the wailing!
Lord of prosperity before the killing of the eighteen,
liberal lord, lone hero ordering battle,
brave lord, like a lion directing the world,
    a lord always restless to destroy,
lord of lucky ventures, before leaving his splendour;
    no Englishman would dare to provoke him.

A lord who was roofstone where the Welsh gather,
   of the line which should hold sway in Aberffraw.
Lord Christ, how grieved I am for him!
True lord, deliverance came by him.
His fall came from the heavy sword-stroke,
from the long swords crushing him down.
By the wound on my king I am dismayed
and the news of the weariness of Bodfaeo's lord.
A complete man was killed by a hostile hand;
   every privilege of his forefathers was his,
candle of kingship, strong lion of Gwynedd,
   chair of honour; there was need of him.
For the death of all Britain, a deathsong for the leader,
for the killing of Nancoel's lion, of Nancaw's shield.
Many a sliding tear runs down the cheek,
   many a flank is red and torn,
much blood has soaked about the feet,
many a widow shrieks for him,
many a sad mind now breaks down,
many a son's left fatherless,
many a homestead stained in the fire's path
   and many a wilderness left by the plunderer,
many a piteous cry, as once at Camlan,
many a tear has fallen down the cheek!
For the killing of our prop, our golden-handed king,
for Llywelyn's death, I remember no one.
The heart is chilled under a breast of fear,
lust shrivels like dry branches.
See you not the way of the wind and the rain?
See you not the oaks beat together?
See you not the sea stinging the land?
   See you not the truth equipping?
See you not the sun sailing the sky?
   See you not the stars have fallen?
Do you not believe God, demented men?
   See you not that the world is in danger?
A sigh to you, God, that the sea may come over the land!
   Why are we left to linger?
There's no retreat from the prison of fear,

there's nowhere to dwell, alas for the dwelling!
There is no counsel, no lock, no opening,
   no way of delivery from terror's sad counsel.
Each retinue was worthy of him
and every warrior stayed about him,
every dogged one swore by his hand,
every ruler, every province was his;
every district, every homestead's invaded,
every clan and line now falls.
The weak and strong were kept by his hand,
every child now weeps in his cradle.
Little good it did me to be tricked
into leaving my head on, with no head on him.
A head which, falling, made panic welcome;
a head which, falling, made it better to give up;
a soldier's head, a head for praise henceforth;
a leader's head, a dragon's head was on him,
head of fair, dogged Llywelyn; it shocks the world
   that an iron stake should pierce it.
My lord's head, a harsh-falling pain is mine,
my soul's head, which has no memorial;
a head which owned honour in nine hundred lands,
   with the homage of nine hundred feasts;
a king's head, iron flew from his hand;
a king's head, a proud hawk breaching a gap;
a regal head of a thrusting wolf,
may the head of heaven be his patron!
A magnificent lord, a blessed host with him;
splendidly eager to voyage to Brittany.
True regal king of Aberffraw,
may Heaven's blessed kingdom be his abode!

20. *Thief of Love*

Eight times I've gone (quick-wounding words)
to yonder woods on fruitless errands;
I was like a madman out of doors,
watching a house but with no fire.
By God, I find it easy
(may it succeed!) before dawn comes
to retreat to the wood's far side,
eagerly, for the sake of a girl.
Dawn in the woods annoys me,
a man walking to a far love.
I am desperate, I am ruined
by the sun of the woods, which once poured wine.
If from a house they see me running
in the pain-paying region of the fair girl,
I'm there, in a fighting net,
an arrant thief, says the grey-cheeked churl.
But I'm no stable-loft thief,
avoiding day's bright face.
I am a thief, a wound binds me,
thief of a fair girl, not a black stallion;
for tonight no thief of a ram,
thief of a maiden this happy time;
no thief of a cattle enclosure,
thief of her, wave-coloured, in the fair wood;
thief of a strange, bold enchantress,
not of a fulling mill, but an anxious journey;
agonised thief of a girl who's not mine,
thief of pure love, no thief of purses;
no thief of a young hoofed beast,
yet never was a claim so far-reaching upon me.
Stolen love now overcomes me;
shackle of pain, I am the thief of a girl.

21. *The Woodland Mass*

A pleasant place I was at to-day,
under mantles of the worthy green hazel,
listening at day's beginning
to the skilful cock thrush
singing a splendid stanza
of fluent signs and symbols;
a stranger here, wisdom his nature,
a brown messenger who had journeyed far,
coming from rich Carmarthenshire
at my golden girl's command.
Wordy, yet with no password,
he comes to the sky of this valley.
It was Morfudd who sent it,
this metrical singing of May's foster son.
About him was a setting
of flowers of the sweet boughs of May,
like green mantles, his chasuble
was of the wings of the wind.
There was here, by the great God,
nothing but gold in the altar's canopy.
I heard, in polished language,
a long and faultless chanting,
an unhesitant reading to the people
of a gospel without mumbling;
the elevation, on the hill for us there,
of a good leaf for a holy wafer.
Then the slim eloquent nightingale
from the corner of a grove nearby,
poetess of the valley, sings to the many
the Sanctus bell in lively whistling.
The sacrifice is raised
up to the sky above the bush,
devotion to God the Father,
the chalice of ecstasy and love.

The psalmody contents me;
it was bred of a birch-grove in the sweet woods.

22. *The Girls of Llanbadarn*

I bow before this passion;
a plague on the parish girls!
Because, o force of longing,
I've never had one of them!
No sweet and hoped for maiden,
nor young girl, nor hag, nor wife.
What recoiling, what malice,
what lack makes them not want me?
What harm to a fine-browed girl
to have me in the thick dark wood?
It were no shame for her
to see me in a lair of leaves.
No one's been so bewitched
save the men of Garwy's nature,
for no day do I fall in love
with fewer than one or two,
yet no nearer to having one
than if she were my foe.
Each Sunday at Llanbadarn
I've stood, let others witness,
with my face towards the fine girl
and my back to the pure God.
And after my long staring
over my plumed hat and over the people,
one girl says, piercingly clear,
to the other, who's quick to see it,
'The pale fellow with the affected look
and his sister's hair on his head,
adulterously he glances,
this crooked looker versed in wickedness.'
'Do you think he's pretending?'
says the other girl at her side.
'He'll never get an answer;
let the fool get out to the Devil!'

The bright girl's curse amazes me,
small payment for one dazed with love;
and it's made me abandon
these ways, these visions of terror.
I'd best become a hermit,
a villain's occupation.
O strange lesson, through too much looking
over my shoulder, a picture of weakness
I became, this lover of powerful song,
wry headed and companionless.

23. *The Rattle Bag*

Upon a day (o easiest praise!)
in summer, when I found myself
under green trees between mountain and meadow
in ambush for my soft-worded girl,
she came, I'll not deny it,
the undoubted moon, to the promised place.
We sat together (splendid theme!)
not yet agreed, the girl and I,
and whilst this freedom was still mine
I conferred with the excellent girl.
Whilst we were thus, and she still shy,
realizing each other's love,
hiding the wrong and finding mead,
lying together the space of an hour,
there came, cold food for pining,
with a cry, a foul performance,
a sorry little boiling sound from a bag's bottom,
from some beast in the form of a shepherd.
He had with him, notorious evil,
a nasty, shrivel-cheeked, dry-horned rattle bag.
He played this yellow-paunched prowler,
this rattle bag with its scabbed shank.
And so, before satiety,
the worthy girl took fright,
for when she of the frail-wounded breast
heard the winnowed stones, she stayed no longer.
Under Christ, no Christian accent
with a cold name was ever so harsh;
a sounding bag at a stick's end,
a ringing bell of pebbles and grit,
a stony English instrument singing
quaveringly in a bullock's hide,
a cradle of three thousand chafers,
a hissing cauldron, a black bag,

a meadow guard, a companion of straw,
black-skinned, pregnant with splinters,
whose accent an old roebuck hates,
the devil's bell with a pole in her fork,
scar-crested, stone-bearing pebble-womb,
may it make thongs for buckles!
And a coldness on the scattering churl
(Amen!) who frightened away my girl!

24. The Death of Lleucu Llwyd

It's a sad summer for a lively poet
and a sad world for him.
There is in Gwynedd to-day
nor moon, nor light, nor colour,
since was put (unlucky welcome!)
the moon's beauty under hard earth.
O girl in your oak chest,
my fate is bitter without you.
Fine of form, candle of Gwynedd,
though you be in the grave's keeping,
my soul, bestir yourself,
open the black earth-door,
reject the long bed of gravel
and come to meet me, maiden.
There is here above your grave
(o brief beauty of sunny face!)
a sad-faced man who lacks you,
Llywelyn Goch, bell of your praise,
a wailing poet walking in affliction,
servant to passion's vigour.
O girl of growing excellence,
I was yesterday[1] above your grave
letting fall great streams of tears
in a rope along my face;
but you, fair image of a dumb girl,
gave me no answer from the dark pit,
loveless, profoundly speechless.
O silent girl, sweet-mannered,
bright, pretty one in a silk shroud,
you promised to wait for me
until I came from the south,
and that's the truth, the guard of trust.

[1] Literally, 'The day before yesterday', but this is not so easy to put into a line as the Welsh word *echdoe*.

O straight, unhindered cry, I never heard
a lying word, my silent maiden,
true formed Indeg of girls,
from your sweet lips before.
A great blow to me, and I don't care where
I go, the sadness of your breach of faith.
No, you are true, it is my poem,
with its facile words, that's false.
I'm a liar, my deprivations
I spoke of in a lying voice.
I'll go from Gwynedd to-day
no matter where, bright-coloured one,
my very lively one, and yet
if you still lived, by God, I would not go!
Where shall I, I don't care where,
see you again, my moon-fair girl?
Will it be on Mount Olivet,
where Ovid's love is trampled on?
You have made sure my place,
Lleucu, of the fine colour of the fair wave,
dear-bright, fair-shining girl
oversleeping within your stone walls.
Get up to end the banquet,
to see whether you'd like a grave,¹
to your poet who no longer laughs
any more because of you, my gold chaplet.
Come, you of the cheeks of rose,
up from the gloomy earth-house!
A wilderness is the track,
this is the truth, of my true feet
walking to and fro in the cold
about your house, Lleucu Llwyd.
All the poetry I have sung,
lantern of Gwynedd, snow-featured,
gold-ringed hand, each triple-sighed cry
was praise of you, Lleucu my gold.
These lips know how to praise;
the praise I'll sing whilst I'm alive,
my soul, my love, my river-ripple colour,

¹ "*a fynnych fedd*" can here also mean "whether you'd like mead", an intended
ambiguity.

57

shall be your funeral song.
My dainty, clear, bright Lleucu,
my loved one's legacy was this:
her soul, Meirionnydd's jewel,
to God the Father, a proper promise;
and her sweet body of fine flour hue
virgin to the saint's holy ground;
a faultless person, flour-white gifts
and the world's wealth to her black, proud husband;
and she left to me my longing
for her, the vexation in my song.
O mournful custom, two equal gifts
of earth and stone and oak now hide
her cheeks, the jewel of my bitter woe,
sweet Lleucu, of driven-snow colour.
Woe's me, the weight of gravel
and earth on beauty's mistress!
Woe's me, a coffin guards you
and a stone house between us two!
Woe is me, fair girl of Pennal,
and hateful dream that your brow should be earthed!
A hard oak case, o bitter sad lot,
and earth, o fair of feature,
and a heavy door, a heavy barrier,
a floor of field between her form and me,
a sheltering wall, a black steel lock
and a latch; goodbye, my Lleucu!

25. *The Labourer*

When the world's folk, one day of freedom,
the lively host of Christendom,
show their works before God
the beloved Lord (fine true words)
on the great mountain of Olivet,
where they will all be judged,
the labourer, the meadow traveller,
will tell a simple, cheerful tale.
The lively God is generous;
if a man has given God offering and tithe,
then a good soul directly
he'll pay to God and merit bliss.
The worker in the bright meadow
easily trusts to the Lord God.
Most properly his almsgiving
and hospitality are for all.
He'll speak his mind only on ploughs;
he hates dissension where he works.
He'll make and follow no war,
he'll oppress no one for his goods,
he's never brutal with us
nor will he pursue false claims.
Suffering is his seemly way,
yet there's no life without him.
He finds it many times pleasanter,
and I think no worse of him,
to grip in his placid way
the crooked plough and the goad
than if he were wrecking a tower
in the guise of a ravaging Arthur.
Without his work there's no
Christ's sacrifice to feed our faith,
and without him no pope
or emperor can keep alive,

no wine-giving, sprightly king
of notable prudence, no living man.
The useful old Elucidarium
put it thus happily,
'Blessed is he who through his youth
holds in his hands the plough.'
It's a cradle tearing the smooth long broom,
a fishing basket lacing the field,
a holy image of dear praise,
a heron opening a quick furrow,
a basket for the wild earth, now to be tamed
in honoured, coultered order;
a gander of the wild acres,
grain will come of its true skill.
It fetches crops from the rich earth,
it's a good beast biting the ground.
It must have its knife and its board
and its food right under its thigh.
It goes unwillingly through stones,
it skins the field with leg outstretched.
It's head is ever employed
on a fair way beneath oxen's feet.
It has often sung its hymn,
it loves to follow the plough chain.
A root-breaker of valley growth,
it stretches a stiff neck out;
tough-headed train-bearer,
its wooden shank scatters the earth.
Hu Gadarn, lord of a lively people,
a king who gave wine for verse,
emperor of land and seas,
Constantinople's golden constable,
after defeat took up
the nimble, fine-beamed plough,
for this hale, host-scattering lord,
this great leader never sought bread
but, so well instructed was he,
by his own labour. This gifted eagle
wished to show to the proud

and to the wisely humble that
in the sight of the Father of the holy relic
one craft was best, a sign of triumph,
that ploughing is a scholarship.
Where there's belief and baptism
and everyone upholding the faith,
the Lord God's hand on this best of men
and Mary's hand on every labourer.

26. Sir Hywel of the Axe

Would anyone see what I see
in the night (I'll make amends)
when, in the greatest pain that is,
I sleep as an old man sleeps?
For first I truly see
a fine great sea-fronting fort,
with a splendidly built keep,
men on the platforms, a rampart,
and the blue sea at its fair stone base,
with foam to the swelling of the blue-grained tower,
the song of fifes and bagpipes,
and a joyful lord, a notable man;
then girls, far from unlively,
weaving the shining, lovely silk;
proud men at the fort's high table
playing backgammon and chequers;
a pale, grey man, the boar of battle,
wild-natured, gives me his sweet wine
in finest golden goblet
thus from his hand into mine;
and a fine long black standard
above the tower (a good soldier was he),
with three white worthy flowers
of the same form, with silver leaves.
Strange that there is no elder
in Gwynedd's great feasting land
who is now able to tell me
whether I am where I wish to be.
One answers, 'Yes, proud fellow,
you're dreaming over there.
The fair wall that you see,
the good homestead you'd come to,
the bright fort on its height of rock
and the red rock at the croft corner,

this is Cricieth of fine structure,
it's that old citadel.
The grey man, the great spear-shatterer,
is Sir Hywel, lightning's mangonel,
with his wife of golden girdle,
Sir Hywel, lord of needful war,
and her fair-skinned handmaidens,
ranged there twelve by twelve,
weaving the bright-hued fair silk
in the shafts of the sun through worthy glass.
And in your vision you saw
a standard of splendid sort:
this is Sir Hywel's streamer
and, by Beuno, in this pennon
are three fleur-de-lys embroidered
proudly in their sable ground.'
The nature of bloody-speared Gruffudd's son
led him to his enemies
to sharpen his lance in their blood
savagely, this golden-footed lord,
carver of battle, fine red H,
speedy to war, the bloody shield,
tusks of a fearful boar,
an old backbone to us in our need.
When he put (what a check for pomp!)
a bridle on the French King's head,
he was a barber like Erbin's son,
with lance and sword, both heavy in battle;
he shaved, with his hand and strength,
the heads and beards he met,
letting flow, as fast as he could,
blood over feet, a grief for some.
He will be loved by the gentle romancer,[1]
his poets are many, his table's praised.
He's warden, an eighteen-pointed stag,
and keeper of the huddled town;
a brave warhorse keeping the garrison,
long will he keep the land.

[1] Who may Einiort be unless Eilhart? Iolo's knowledge and interests are wide and unpredictable.

He'll protect the people in his strong seat,
he'll hold the castle, he's better than an army,
he'll hold two frontiers, this keeper of Longchamps;
he'll hold the two lands and war and its reward;
he'll keep the walrus at the shore,
he'll keep the tides, the halls, the land;
he'll hold all lands and the bright tower,
he'll hold the fort: health to the man!

27. The Illusion of this World

Its purpose hidden, the world is like
an image painter with his brush
painting many images
and a host of saints in star colour.
Like a fat-bellied magician
casting a spell, to a fervent, brave warrior
it shows something where nothing is,
worthless stuff which is bought dear.
That's this world, I know it well,
magic and colour; our work's of no avail.

Where's all the world? It's been a deceiver.
Where's Adam, the first man?
Where's Rulling,[1] Constantinople's king?
Where are the two great popes and their retinues?
Where's Julius, King of Sicily;
the poets of Europe and a thousand more?
Alexander has perished,
and Hector and Arthur, that's clear.
Where's Guinevere, gossamer-featured,
daughter of giant Gogfran of great dominion,
and the silk that was so wonderful
and the hair full of beads of fitting gold?
Where now will marvellous Tegwedd be,
the love of Owain Cyfeiliog?
Where's Vivien, the slim golden armful
from France, whose face was fairest?
Where's Herod, of famous cruelty?
Where's Charlemagne of the vanguard party?
Where's young Basil? Where is Moses?
Where's Brutus, son of old Julius?
Where's Owain, the slim-waisted lord?
Where is King Richard? Where are the ages?

[1] I have failed to trace Rulling and simply anglicise the name.

65

Where are the generous ones and their concerns?
Where are the worthies of old Wales,
the house-holders? Where's the reverence
which as a youth belonged to me?
No credible messenger,
no herald of the wind knows where they are.
The same dance, I hear it come,
will without doubt be ours.
We gather a fortune, a fool's task;
magic and colour, our work's of no avail.

David was most unchaste;
wise Solomon's day was vile.
It echoes over salutation,
York's Duke would give a girl a mark.
Where are they and their women to-day,
their great splendour, their fine mead?
Where are the spells, where the wise ones,
where the seven arts and their fame?
Where's the wise Cato, and Catiline,
and the helpful, seven-wisdomed Virgil?[1]
In spite of his wisdom, people say,
and the great science of his speech
and his tricks and huckstering,
to earth, a tame weakling, he went.
Though those bad men were brave,
strangely proud and demanding,
quite clearly, though strong, they went
as nothing into earth.
From earth we came to our testing;
to earth, though we mourn it, we must go.
Useless to man is love of goods,
his daring and playfulness,
with a battered body and forehead,
with a weight of earth, a tunic of wood,
and, if they tell me truly,
eight hundred worms tasting him.
Earth's seed is now in two lengths;
magic and colour, our work's of no avail.

[1] Virgil was more famous as a wizard than as a poet in the Middle Ages.

O avenging pain of faith! When Christ
comes to the open castle gate
one Sunday as infallible judge
of good and bad, at that sad door
some will cringe like a beaten boy,
some will be gay and merry;
some will receive all heaven,
some pain, excess of punishment.
Then, Lord of worthy Death, shall we see
magic and colour, that our work's of no avail.

28. To a Girl

I'm a man walking the night,
a snug house would be happier;
a stupid man late walking;
for this may God give him sense!
Cold night is black upon me:
God, your help, how black the night!
Sorry little wretch under a wall,
there was never a colder face.
Wake up, girl, protect my soul,
a weary, godly man's under your wall.
Give, you'll get threefold payment,
your garment as alms to the weak,
your lodging, your hand towards me,
your lovely body, say, shall I have it?
Your sweet word from your nobleness,
your lip, like a drink of mead?
Your nurture, gaiety and pleasure,
your slim brow have ruined me.
Your flowing hair, your bilberry brow,
your eye is as dark as your eyebrow!
Your colouring like monks' vestments,
black and white, bewitches men;
your face like last night's snow,
your blush a bunch of roses.
I have loved loving you:
no Englishman would be so cruel to me.
Sadly I bear your song,
under eaves vainly singing.
Pass your kind mother's kerchief
through the window to roof my head!
Your song will I sing everywhere
and not despair of your requiting.
I love you to my sorrow;
you courtly and I artless.

Your precincts are well locked,
you're lovely; may God be about you!
Sadly I bear your poem,
I've been ill-treated, give me a kiss!
Your counsel against urgent wrath
will be good, and your consent, my Gwen.

29. *A Girl's Hair*

He who could win the girl I love
would win a grove of light,
with her silken, starry hair
in golden columns from her head,
dragon fire lighting up a door,
three chains like the Milky Way?
She sets alight in one bush
a roof of hair like a bonfire.
Yellow broom or a great birch tree
is this gold-topped girl of Maelor.
A host coloured like angels,
her armour's many-branched,
a peacock-feather pennon,
a tall bush like the golden door,
all this lively looking hair
virtued like the sun, fetter of girls.
Anyone would know, were he a goldsmith,
who owns this fine strong hair.
In summer she has on her head
something like the Golden Hillside.
This fair growth is the girl's garment,
a tent for the sun, or harp strings,
ears of corn closed in above,
reed peelings as ornaments for the breast;
a peahen constantly carrying
hair of broom from head to ground,
a noose of woven amber,
the gold of corn like twig-chains;
her hair's a tree-high woodland,
a twig-crown of new wax.
Labour of bees has ripened
the seeds of warmth from a girl's flesh,
saffron on the herb eyebright,

cherries of gold, like the stars of night.
A good band round its coming growth,
fresh water-grass, golden water-hair,
lye water wets it like sweet herbs;
yellow-hammer head, bush of silk;
a sheaf of Mary Magdalen's broom
is the gold band that binds her hair.
If we let it down all glowing,
she'll wear a gown of golden hair.
It covers her two breasts
from its roof of gold in two fathoms,
fair ringlets, load of a girl's head,
flax before bush of yellow.
If spread out, the bush is gold:
was ever bush so yellow?
In order that from the christening font
the oil of faith should mark her head,
giving life to the sun's bush,
there's no such bush now under the sun.

30. *Naming the Girl*

The great warmth of a maiden's love
has me captive night and day;
loving a girl with a long bright neck
and keeping it a secret.
From her lips I get wine,
her smile enfeebles me.
If they took all time to name her,
yet no man would know her.
Annes first will I name;
I get a pact and a refusal
from a fine girl in colour and form;
yes, she may well be Enid.
Sweet pensive Guinevere,
Gwladus of the sugared lip,
Catherine, Gwenllian I'll greet,
Cari, Mallt, the properest girl,
Lleucu of hill primrose hue,
Lowri under green branches.
Soft is Myfanwy's kiss;
I'm at death's door for Gweirful;
Margaret's faith is mine,
she brings far-brought red gold.
I beat my cheek and keep my faith,
I love kissing my Janet;
wild and low is my look,
lying with Tegwedd has charmed me.
I'm weak, there's a pain in my skull,
my pain for Angharad grows greater.
There's an arrow in her deep bosom
which won't be drawn in a meteor's life.
A star under gold rushes of hair,
I spy out Alison for the wood.
In the woods there is white trefoil,
a green birch tree and Morfudd.

Alis, Isabel, Helen,
Eva or Nêst is my bright girl.
All these have now been named,
and one of these is the girl.

31. *The Death of Siôn Eos*

It's hard for those left behind,
the trouble of a chance enmity;
the smallest of all crimes,
but the best man in all our tongue.
O men, why isn't it better,
if one is killed, not to kill two?
He took one enemy's blood,
avenged our dual enmity.
It was sad, the killing of two good men
for such a little cause!
He wounded, there's no denying,
but never meant to kill the man.
Somebody was at fault
for striking back in a chance mêlée.
Contention for generations
and the suffering that came between the two;
and so one man was killed
and vengeance takes the other.
Even if body paid for body
compensation would be better for the soul.
Then came the promises—
his weight in gold to save Siôn's life.
I hate the churlish law
of the Chirk Lordship; it took a nightingale away.
O Lordship, why not under seal
apply Hywel's law to your Nightingale?
When they had put upon him
the fullness of London's law,
they would not, for his life's sake,
lay bare a relic or make the sign of the cross.
And so they doomed to death
the man who was father of music;
the twelve were all agreed,
fair God, on the man's life.

Now Siôn's gone, there's no good sense
in music, nor master of it.
An arm felled the tree-top nightingale's tower;
the measure of music's foot was broken,
the steps to the house of descant were broken,
learning was broken like a string breaking.
Is there from Ewyas to Anglesey
learning left fit for learners?
Rheinallt himself doesn't know
and yet he sings a man's part;
his fellow has fallen silent
and Teirtu's harp is shattered.
You now are silent too,
golden harp of the harpists.
Each finger-nail held a string,
keys of the male voice or base note,
a meditation between thumb and finger,
mean and sweet treble from three fingers.
Is there, now Nightingale's gone,
his equal at playing a prelude,
an improvisation and manly song,
an air in a nobleman's presence?
What maker now in music
has anything but what he made?
Distastefully, I know no concord
without the song of music's Nightingale.
There is no angel or man
who'd not weep at his harp-playing.
O, let it not be played tonight,
now that its master is doomed!
Men of Chirk, their judgement won't avail
against the musician at Heaven's gate!
And if their judgement was just,
may the same doom fall upon them;
it's he who'll go to life,
not changing worlds at their verdict.
The life of my man is now night;
God's life to John Nightingale!

32. *From Lent to Summer*

The jealous husband's day of bliss
came yesterday to plague me;
Shrove-tide's a day that weighs
like the world's end on a poet.
The way to heaven opens,
God leads men under their loads;
forty days of forgiveness
there are for saintly prayers.
Lord, every single day
was doled out like a year.
Three days of this, an outlaw's fate,
are long for the world I live in.
The anchorite's faith from Rome
becomes mine, like an author of prayers;
in their faith I'm correct,
the girl's correct, she'll love,
giving us, like Fridays,
lenten tasks to subdue us.
Goodbye, my little slimwaist,
everyone's chaste till Easter Monday.
I'll not see her, nor for her leave
the house one night till then.
I'll not beg for a kiss, my dear,
nor anything for my bashful soul.
When Easter comes with its green trees,
the girl will meet me daily.
Is not the payment made through Easter
a covenant for damask wearing?
Then will come our day
with its plenitude of joy,
May and summer, where she is
and cuckoos like Gwgon's daughter;
each birchgrove in fine hair,

a green coat and a weight of hair,
and on the street of thorn stems
linen shops like London's Cheap;
herbs and dew in gardens,
berries for wine, ridges of wheat,
a clear sky, a blue-capped sea,
a snug screen in a green grove,
a lonely place in a glade
and a slim branch of a girl.
Then we'll end all our penance,
ebb out the pain and spin the world
and henceforth put our curses
on the chilly, windy Spring.

33. On the Death of his Son

One son was a jewel to me:
o Dwynwen, his father bewails his birth!
I have been left pain for love,
to ache for ever without a son.
My plaything is dead and my sides
are sick for Siôn y Glyn.
I moan continually
for a little story-book chieftain.
A sweet apple and a bird
the boy loved, and white pebbles,
a bow made of a thorn twig
and little brittle swords of wood.
He feared a pipe and a scarecrow
and begged his mother for a ball.
He'd sing for anyone,
singing io-o for a nut.
He'd make as though to flatter
and then fall out with me;
then make it up for a chip of wood
or a dice that he desired.
O, that Siôn, sweet innocent,
could live again like Lazarus.
Beuno brought seven heaven-dwellers
back again into this life.
Woe upon woe to my true heart
that Siôn's soul does not make eight.
O Mary, woe for his lying down
and woe to my side for the closing of his grave!
Siôn's death stands near me
like two barbs in my breast.
My son, child of my hearth,
my breast, my heart, my song,
my one delight before my death,
my knowing poet, my luxury.

my jewel, and my candle,
my sweet soul, my one betrayal,
my chick learning my song,
my chaplet of Iseult, my kiss,
my nest, (woe that he's gone!)
my lark, my little wizard.
My Siôn, my bow, my arrow,
my suppliant, my boyhood,
Siôn sends to his father
a sharpness of longing and love.
No more smiles for my lips,
no more laughter from my mouth,
no more sweet entertainment,
no more begging for nuts,
no longer any playing ball
and no more singing aloud.
Farewell, whilst I live below,
my merry darling, Siôn, my son.

34. *To Ask for a Stallion*

On Conwy bank have I been feasted
by one who is keeper of Gwynedd,
an abbot over eight regions,
Aberconwy's vine enclosure,
a lord who freely gives feasts,
doubly a habit at an abbot's table;
spices in one man's dish,
oranges in another's.
Conwy, in a temperate valley,
the river's verge where I get pure wine;
Grwst's Vale and fair Caer Awstin,
green valley of the gallons of wine;
three times worth the prince's kitchen,
the work turns heavily on his cook;
houses for wine, mead-temples,
a trestl and a trim buttery.
At once on all his wines
he has been head in every tongue.
Where would I go for saintly sessions?
To him and his fellow monks,
men numbered in Rome's people,
white and crimson are their gowns.
If his bosom and cope are white,
dressed thus he'll make a bishop,
and thus he'd go in fine miniver
on trial to be Pope of Rome.
It's irksome work and folly
to strive for patronage.
They asked a thousand petty rents;
he asked for that of Maenan.
This man's support is like tree-bloom
over Meirionnydd's face.

Lewis, son of Madoc, boldly
will now ask for a stallion.
He's a soldier between Maelor and Rhos,
and closely linked with Tegeingl.
He wishes to have, ready for May,
a pretty girl and a horse to carry her.
For a poem he seeks one with a stag's look,
a dimple-nosed one turning in his tunic,
a bear's nostril, a moving mouth,
a bridle holding his nose in a loop,
a nose which holds the bridle when we curb him,
the hollow nostril like the muzzle of a gun.
Eyes that are like two pears,
lively and keen, they leap in his head;
two slim and restless ears,
like sage leaves at his forehead;
like polishing of gems
was the glazier's dressing of his hooves;
brisk on four sets of eight nails,
with a spark from every nail's head.
His coat is like new silk,
his hair might be tree gossamer,
silk of a skylark's tunic
and camlet covering a young stag.
He spins without use of hands
and weaves a kerchief of silk.
Strong-waisted foal biting the highway,
the fair's alarm, out of his way!
His liveliness we liken
to a red fawn before the hounds.
He's such a lusty creature
that he floats to his purpose;
to make him prance you'll never
need to put steel to his belly;
under a brisk, keen horseman
he always knows his mind;
leaping over where thorns are greatest,
full of attack in Llan Eurgain.
If he's ridden over to the hayfield

he won't break eight stalks with his hoof.
Stirring to the thunder's course,
and mincingly stepping when he pleases,
he'd throw a leap at the sky,
he'd fly confidently,
and if we ride him over a wall
this prince's horse will run on.
A battering ram winding up the hill,
he throws his nailheads to the sun;
sparks fly from every hoof,
eight points are pierced into each one;
there are stars or lightning on the road
at the lifting of his fetlocks.
Like a stag with fiercest gaze,
his feet weave through wild fire;
he jumps across a river
like a roebuck jumping from a snake.
Is there better payment for such a fawn
than praise of the slim beast?
There's a maiden, a beauty waiting for me,
if I had a horse to carry her off.
The best speed ever made was by
a good horse bearing a pretty girl.

35. *To a Sweet-mouthed Girl*

Sweet, pure, proper, sugared mouth, I know
    a snug grip for lip-locking.
    My pretty one of the shining brow,
    her lips are like clear honey.

Like honey the grip of her lip, sweet,
    pure, loving jewel,
    loveliest girl of all islands,
    whitest skin under flour-white shift.

Sweet is her lip and her grip on the harp string,
    she would tempt any angel.
    She is most sweetly vocal
    and best at the low harmony.

36. Longing

Longing! leave my heart for an hour
    and turn away awhile
  to tell my yellow-topped girl
    that here's a man for whom the world is vile.

37. Three Hinds of Denbighshire

My day, my news, my night, my mind,
    my forgiveness, you're near me
and I am waiting meekly.
Even if you'll be my enemy, come.

All joy, all empty jollity, all thought,
    every mannerly companion,
everything indeed but longing
has suddenly gone away from me.

There's a river, a hillside and fresh boughs of trees
    that hide three hinds.
Today no hunter finds
them, or tries their willing flesh.

The morning you'll be ready, concerned
    with deer hunting:
not one prey are we proposing,
but a notable group of three.

Not with dogs should you decide to hunt us—
    that wouldn't be luckiest;
better for you, my love, to tryst
under trees with your dogs tied.

38. Stanzas to the Harp

Set golden fingers for a moment to the harp,
    against hurt and displeasure;
  soft music's cheering measure
  most fittingly removes your torment.

For the plucked strings' melody, the music,
    the themes without number,
  I'll follow the harp for ever,
  for it is rich in tracery.

From the song of the tuned string, the hint
    of high treble and pipe chord,
  descanting to its grave concord
  the voice will bring us solacing.

39. Marchan Wood

A poem on behalf of the squirrels who went to London to file and make an affidavit on the bill for the cutting down of Marchan Wood, near Rhuthyn.

Odious and hard is the law
and painful to little squirrels.
They go the whole way to London
with their cry and their matron before them.
This red squirrel was splendid,
soft-bellied and able to read;
she conversed with the Council
and made a great matter of it.
When the Book was put under her hand
in the faith that this would shame her,
she spoke thus to the bailliff,
'Sir Bribem, you're a deep one!'
Then on her oath she said,
'All Rhuthyn's woods are ravaged;
my house and barn were taken
one dark night, and all my nuts.
The squirrels all are calling
for the trees; they fear the dog.
Up there remains of the hill wood
only grey ash of oak trees;
there's not a stump unstolen
nor a crow's nest left in our land.
The owls are always hooting
for trees; they send the children mad.
The poor owl catches cold,
left cold without her hollow trunk.
Woe to the goats, without trees or hazels,
and to the sow-keeper and piglets!
Pity an old red-bellied sow
on Sunday, in her search for an acorn.

The chair of the wild cats,
I know where that was burnt.
Goodbye hedgehog! No cow-collar
nor pig-trough will come from here any more.
If a plucked goose is to be roasted,
it must be with bracken from Rhodwydd Gap.
No pot will come to bubbling,
no beer will boil without small twigs;
and if peat comes from the mountain
in the rain, it's cold and dear.
Colds will exhaust the housemaid,
with cold feet and a dripping nose.
There's no hollow trunk or branch,
nor a fence for the beating of an old thin snipe.
Yes, Angharad spoke the truth,
if we don't get coal it's goodbye to our land.'

40. Glyn Cynon Wood

Aberdare, Llanwynno through,
all Merthyr to Llanfabon;
there was never a more disastrous thing
than the cutting of Glyn Cynon.

They cut down many a parlour pure
where youth and manhood meet;
in those days of the regular star
Glyn Cynon's woods were sweet.

If a man in sudden plight
took to flight from foe,
for guest-house to the nightingale
in Cynon Vale he'd go.

Many a birch-tree green of cloak
(I'd like to choke the Saxon!)
is now a flaming heap of fire
where iron-workers blacken.

For cutting the branch and bearing away
the wild birds' habitation
may misfortune quickly reach
Rowenna's treacherous children!

Rather should the English be
strung up beneath the seas,
keeping painful house in hell
than felling Cynon's trees.

Upon my oath, I've heard it said
that a herd of the red deer
for Mawddwy's deep dark woods has left,
bereft of its warmth here.

No more the badger's earth we'll sack
nor start a buck from the glade;
no more deer-stalking in my day,
now they've cut Glyn Cynon's shade.

If ever a stag got into a wood
with huntsmen a stride behind,
never again will he turn in his run
with Cynon Wood in mind.

If the flour-white girl once came
to walk along the brook,
Glyn Cynon's wood was always there
as a fair trysting nook.

If as in times gone by men plan
to span the mountain river;
though wood be found for house and church
Glyn Cynon's no provider.

I'd like to call on them a quest
of every honest bird,
where the owl, worthiest in the wood,
as hangman would be heard.

If there's a question who rehearsed
in verse this cruel tale,
it's one who many a tryst has kept
in the depth of Cynon Vale.

41. The Trial of Cresyd

(Sinon, Calcas' servant, rushing in to Priaf, King of
Troy, and his council)

SINON   All pleasure to your honour!
Lord Calcas has escaped
suddenly in the night
to the company of the Greeks.
My lords, you must guard yourselves
against deceit through trusting.
A dear and only daughter
is Cresyd to this Calcas,
but she won't take upon her
her loss or his iniquity.
It's likely that she knew
all about his departure.

PRIAF   Away you go quickly
and bring this traitor's daughter
to face her punishment.
(turning to his sons)
My sons, unless we see
quickly to these things
and to this kindled fire
whilst it can be put out,
we shall be face to face
with much more treachery.
An ample punishment
must be inflicted for this,
otherwise I fear
a great increase of evil
and Helenus' forebodings
will turn to bitter truth.

(CRESYD comes in with SINON and falls upon
her knees)

CRESYD   My gracious lordships, you
          have caused me to be fetched
          in anger and displeasure.
          I fear adversity.

PRIAF   Are you the only daughter
          of Calcas, uncivil churl,
          who would sell his honour
          at his old age's end
          in order to betray
          his renowned country
          by going to the captivity
          of strangers' company?
          Your conscience and your custom
          indict your falsity,
          for you are to be held guilty
          of all his wickedness.
          From his great wrong and treachery
          ruin may fall upon his land.
          Therefore with you first,
          Cresyd, will I begin.
          Your blood and your existence,
          your penance, your great pain
          and your most cruel death
          will tranquillize my heart.
          What do you say, my lords?
          What death shall we put on her?

PARIS   Send her to be burnt
          for her false viciousness.
          Death, that is to say.
          See that the law's fulfilled!

ENEAS   No, cause her to be thrown
          into a deep, dark pit.
          Burning is far too clean
          for such iniquity.

ANTENOR   Let her be thrown tonight

into the lions' cave;
at least she'd make one meal
for those hungry beasts.

HELENUS Put her in a prison-house
to suffer gloom and sadness,
to waste her life away,
grieving within her prison.

HECTOR Send her off to the Greeks
after the old traitor!
Wherever this girl goes
she'll do but little harm.

TROELUS On the innocent take no vengeance
for the misdeed of the guilty.
and don't be over hasty,
she may be innocent.

CRESYD Oh, my gracious lords,
don't set your hearts so much
on spilling innocent blood
for another's evil deeds.
If Calcas caused you pain,
Cresyd was without malice.
His is the guilty answer
and mine is innocence.
The father culpable
and the daughter punished,
that's a detestable law
and much against your honour.
If he had made me party
to his treacherous defection,
I should not be within reach,
lingering amidst a war,
with soldiers passing by
frequently where I am,
and I a lonely maiden.
A girl can only lament!

My lords, he knew he couldn't
put his trust in me
and that's the reason why
he fled so suddenly.
My wish is that my life,
by suffering want and pain,
could fully compensate
for this most terrible deed,
that this cause might not be
a shame upon my nation.
Then, lords, I'd not be begging
you now to give me pardon.
(TROELUS *whispers in his brother* HECTOR'S *ear*)

TROELUS Hector, my dear brother,
defender of poor innocence,
I call upon your greatness
here to defend the truth.
Be a defence for Cresyd,
the saving of her life.

HECTOR I beg of you to listen
to this pitiful weeping
and to take mercy on
this innocent girl's complaint.
If she had been made party
to his treacherous going,
it would be natural
for her to keep it secret,
for this most terrible thing
would cost her father's life.
If you behave thus cruelly
what will our enemies say?
'Where there's such cruelty
there can't be bravery.'

TROELUS (*and now he falls in love*)
I will pledge my life
that there's no evil in her,

nor ever any practice
of treachery or deceit.
We now petition you
to be forgiving to her
and henceforth, from this hour
will I, Troelus, myself
pledge all my liberty
for Cresyd's honesty.
(TROELUS *turns to* SINON *who had accused her,*
whispering)
You lying rottenness,
eager for all informing,
your swaggering device
is to lead lies around
and put the blame on innocence
with your imagined malice
and to excuse the evil
of your own blemished living
by shaking of your tail
on every kind of person.
Were it not for the presence
of my true natural father,
by all the gods that are
I'd put my sword through you!

PRIAF   Your plea is not opposed
even though Asia be lost.
Go, Cresyd, in innocence
and give thanks to my sons.
Let us go in to meditate
on what is more to do.

HECTOR   (*to* CRESYD *when the others have left*)
Go back now to your home
and leave all heaviness.
Take up your liberty
happily, and your life.
And put your trust in me
to the utmost of my power.

42. *In Defence of Woman*

Let all the nations listen
from the meadows and the mountains
where a satire was made public
against girls and women
for the ill of their behaving
in the beginning of ages.

If you contemplate and render
all books and every story,
not one was born in any age
to be named without her sin;
they merit justice, there's no doubt,
without God's heavenly mercy.

But before judging let all read
the eighth chapter of John,
where God quickly said to those
that brought a woman to him,
who most sadly had transgressed
against Christ himself;

to them Jesus said, 'Let
him of you who is without sin
raise a stone and fist
to kill by covenant.'
The whole land was guilty rather
and God the Father knew it.

To the woman he said softly,
'Go thou in faithfulness
and use no sin hereafter.'
To the multitude his charge was,
none should rashly make judgement,
that moment had not come.

He reprimanded Eve
for her sin and arrogance,
and from her came Mary
to make recompense,
whose son from the closed furnace
drew all the race of Adam.

Joachim was her father
and Anna, her mother, came
from the old blood of kings,
from the generation of Judah,
from stem of David, prophet of Christ,
a list far from unhappy.

When Mary was three years old
and in Jerusalem
she was made consecrate
to God and his strange works,
that from her by foretelling
might spring the best of men.

Virgin before the gift of Christ
and, pregnant, a rare virgin,
a virgin at his birth
and a virgin suckling him.
Jesus her son upon the tree
paid the fee for man.

Five virtues the Trinity gave
to maids but not to men.
With that in mind it's proper
that we should all acknowledge
gentle woman's progeny
as filling sky and earth.

The first virtue was to create
a girl in paradise,
and she was pure and proper,
as pretty as ever went to church,

but of her sweet tribe not one
will there again be born.

The second virtue was that Christ,
our Lord Jesus and the man
who was intent to save us
and will come to judge us,
should choose birth from a girl's flesh,
whose every wish was loving.

The third heavenly virtue—
to a woman in living flesh
the gracious God appeared
in his true earthly body,
having risen from his stone-capped grave
before the twelve apostles.

The fourth bountiful virtue,
the taking of a physical woman,
her placing in heaven, says wisdom,
under God the chief of peoples.
Where only God and the Word were
this Mary went as Mother.

The fifth famous virtue—
that the retinued Helena
got the blessed miraculous cross
(denied to the armed soldier)
and knew from the three crosses
the true cross of the merciful God.

Mary Magdalen we all know;
though she lived a wanton
yet did God still love her.
She changed through her repentance
and tearfully with her hair
dried the bare feet of Jesus.

Saint Catherine the gracious

for heavenly Jesus' sake
went on the monstrous wheel of steel;
her godly body was broken
and from her breast so frail
came the two oils of the world.

Saint Margaret through prayer,
when the dragon swallowed her,
grew within its jaws
and thus split the dragon.
She came out happily,
in the most seemly fashion.

Caradoc turned to cruelty
when he failed to have Gwenfrewi,
cut off her head and straight there sprang
a well of water, through Christ's might.
Beuno put back her head on her,
upright and fair she lived.

I could never convey
nor name how many girls
the God of Heaven has chosen
to be his saints of light
and to suffer for his sake
pain and ache patiently.

Eliwed's fair and gentle wife
made praise in constant music
for God, redeemer of Christians,
to drown the cruel Pharaoh;
she was shining and fair
and she was Aaron's sister.

When the good prophet David
was weakening in old age,
Abisag was comfort to him
the circuit of seven years in one place
and the slim-browed girl in his bed

was not enjoyed or sullied.

When the innocent Jonas
and the honest Jonathan
were in flight from enemies,
with a basket down a well
Jehosaba, the well-mannered wife,
saved the life of both.

Meek Sarah, daughter of Rachel,
lamenting at her father's bier,
forestalled complaint by marrying
a man to please the vigilant law.
She lived his life out at his side
and she died a virgin.

Rebecca, tranquil lady,
was right in ordering
a covering for her after death,
but though her canopy was good
the listening God chose Peter
to bring her back to walk.

When Lazarus died over there
and was buried in earth
and had been three days in the place,
his flesh beginning to decay,
his sister Martha sought the triple God
to raise his body to life.

Sarah and Rachel were right
not to bear children sadly
to multiply man's race;
they took their handmaidens
to their men, not in deceit
but to get them heirs.

When the prophet David
and Absolom his son each day

struck against each other,
with no concord in the land,
Esther was the good wife whose talk
brought them to walk in peace.

When the firmament (we've all heard it)
was shut against the rain,
Elias the righteous prophet
prayed by counsel of a wife
to temper the world through
and he got dew and rain.

When men of old turned furrows
behind the plough and the chain,
without rest or play
torturing their feet and arms,
Saint Brigid the sweet sister
made seed-spreaders for them.

When the nations were naked
and men wore no clothes,
Palathas the good wife
rapidly invented
a means to spin and weave the wool
till all were fully clothed.

And when the world began
with no herbs or gardens,
Ceres, the best sort of wife,
invented every seed
to garnish the fine food
and give it a good flavour.

A girl called Nicostrata,
of the tribe of Seth and Adam,
out of her greatest learning,
and God's highest grace
devised the origin
of the first Latin letters.

A fair-faced girl called Isis,
a wise one in her living
and sharp in every art
and a great story-teller—
she devised in pictures
the characters of Egypt.

And then there were nine Sibyls,
who made the nine bright books.
One of these girls once came
to the king of the towers of Rome
and asked three hundred talents
of old gold in payment for them.

But the king refused:
the price was far too high.
So she burnt three books
in spite at his refusal
and asked in a firm voice
the same price for the six.

Once more the king refused
and once more three were burnt
in anger at his slowness
and the pain it caused her.
She asked the price, with dignity,
for the three still left.

And so the stubborn king,
(it went to this extreme)
because he failed at the first chance
to take the best of bargains,
with a great cry gave the price of nine
to gain the three remaining.

It is well known that thus
and till the Judgement Day
these books remained in Rome above,
and up and down the country

knowledge and skill to the whole land
was handed from these books.

Justly we praise Cambria
and learn the laws of Marsia:
an honest girl was Susanna,
praiseworthy was Rebecca
and the white-cheeked Semiramis,
the wife of Syria's king.

A woman is fairest in heaven
after the God of Hosts,
on earth and on the seas,
and of all people born
a girl is of flowers the fairest
and noblest in her deeds.

A girl is full of virtues,
in every way she's courteous,
her speech is ever gentle,
her manners sensible,
and prudence in her burns as bright
as in a lighted candle.

A woman is merry and noble
and, like a bee of the woods,
she will make much from little.
She'll keep her husband happy
and as for trysting under the hill,
you'll fare ill if you offer.

If I lived long and healthily
like Moses and like Noah
and wrote never-endingly
each day without idleness,
my love would never let me cease
from praise of woman's beauty.

If he still lived in vanity

who made that bitter satire
without good sense or patience,
without metre or concord of sound,
I'd make him bite his tongue
for the wrong he spoke of women.

If anyone should desire
to plead upon this cause,
let him quietly arise
and say who he is;
he'll get a forceful answer,
the yielder shall cry 'Oh!'

If it is asked and verified
aloud or secretly
who made this fit oration
and rhymed this meditation,
William Cynwal won't deny it
though you cry it through the land.

43. A Poem to show the Trouble that befell him when
he was at Sea.

I followed, o splendid season,
the water over the world to Spain,
thinking that, taking to the sea,
I should come by all treasure.
Wandering, sieving the waters
needily, is the seaman's fate.
I bought a ship, stripped the land
for money for the venture;
victualled it fitly and fair,
victualled where butlers abounded.
I gathered men, a gloomy task,
for utterly vain sea-faring,
some vicious dark-hued Jews,
hell-bellied and abusive.
I took ship to train the men,
then came the need for cursing.
There was a roaring on board,
the master calling muster.
'*Turn the capstan,*' he howled an order,
'*Weigh anchor, all you younkers!*'
A question, '*Where is Meyrick?*'
Then the words, '*Coil the cable quick!*'
Deubott the carpenter's diligent,
'*Assay the pump, you see the pit.*'
'Turn you to fire and be damned!'
'*Trim the ship, whip* to it, yare!
Make haste there, haste, you waster!
Bring in the bowline, you boor!
Bear hard up to throw off plague;
bear aloof if it rain toads!
You, Bunny, fast the bonnet,
sound fine with the line and lead.
Veer the sheet, impotent booby;
about again, if a hundred times!'

Farewell England and dry sand
and Scilly, lovely island.
Roll away with royal wings
to parley off the Burlings.

'*Here's Atkins. Where is Woodcock?*
Bear all night right to the Rock.
Beware of any mishap;
our course is the southern cape.
Take height in all good sense.
Thou Poyns, yonder is the Pole.'

Today we hold in dark tides,
we'll veer away tomorrow.
'You, *Hulling, loose the haliard!*
Off you go along the yard!
Bring near the timber, tomboy!
What cheer? A can of beer, boy!
Munson, hoist up the mainsail.
Be merry, I see a sail.
Give chase, for all I've got!
Out topsail, you lout tipsy!
Give way!' In the winter storm
we mustered and mastered the wind,
starboard and larboard labouring.
'*Clear abaft,* keep clear of trouble!
Port hard the helm, bastard one!
Steady thus, man! Do you hear?
Keep the prize (look out wisely,
hear thou, lad) under thy lee.
Now fire a piece in order.'
Instead, he shot three into her.
'*Shoot again a broadside, gunner!*
We'll be brave if we have her.
Fight for store and leave sorrow,
fear not, shoot the wild fire now!
Lay her aboard!' In all the din,
'*Now enter,* venture over!'

Whilst fighting, open discredit,
we lost our men on the vessel in smoke.
'Give back, lest all be taken!
Is there a means *to save some men?'*
We took an unfortunate day,
we find we mind this Monday,
loudly bewailing fortune's blow,
'O Lord, here is too hard luck!'
Foulk Harry, awkward booby,
is drowned in the battle's din;
Brown Robin Austin withal
is dead, and so is Duddal,
Wenford, Rowland and Winfield,
William and Cobham are killed.
Tom, Meyrick, Dick, each one
is hurt, and so is Horton.
Our ship in grappling so
is *weak and full of leak below,*
and if a storm now takes us
we'll be in too hard a state.
'Go to, pain; let's get to port!
Barris, the beer is sour.'

Thus I got a sleep of care
in payment for this venture.
I doubt if Thomas from here
will get home safe from the green sea.
Before I will pillage or part
buy a ship, I'll be a shepherd.

44. *To a Pretty Girl*

I loved a girl, way of obedience,
and there were tears down my cheeks.
If slim-shaped Venus was fair,
truly bright and lovely of face,
fairer and brighter in all the land
is my love, to my distress.
And if Minerva was fair,
or sweet Diana for that matter,
doubly fair in this year
is my love in a corner of leaves.
If long-wisdomed Pallas was splendid,
or Juno, or wise Dido,
sweeter and more splendid the face
of the bright girl who is my love.
If fresh was the silver breast
of Medea or lovely Lucretia,
this one is fairer and trimmer,
my fine-browed one and my true heart.
If lovely Cressid was fair,
with a skin of great tenderness,
tenderer, yet quite unrustic,
is my warm-featured mistress.
If Helen once was fair,
and a fair thing is the jewel of the world,
twice whiter is the face
of my love, above all girls.
Let my pretty one give thanks
upon her knees that she's so beautiful.

45. The Porpoise

Porpoise, swift, trim and handsome,
finely leaping the fair waves,
sea calf with colourful cheek,
make smooth the course of one who weeps.
You are happy when you can be seen,
merry in the wave-top where land ends.
Of fierce look on cold-rimmed face,
a bear's face in the cold flood,
you frisk and shiver like a fever
and then you heave away.
You strive with water, dark toadstool,
you look at it and snort;
it's as though you plough straight through
the foam of brittle waves;
you cut the salt sea open,
you must have the wave's heart.
Swift, lovely one, brave shadow,
skull of the sea, pillion to the strand,
a water-viper hoeing the wave,
with a look that frightens the heart.
White-bellied and good-natured
wanderer of the captive deep,
wild boar of the brine, in urgent mastery
he crosses the sea in a fine great sweep.
Throughout summer, when the weather changes,
he comes rocking along before the storm;
fierce boar, churn of hell-fury,
cross and greedy before the wild tide.
Strapping with gold-crested breastplate,
a fish with a closed tunic;
sea's burden, two-breasted Leviathan,
he slips and catches along the wave's slope.
Saddle of the sea, take a bearing,
steer a course to the loud water,

choose a fathom, go on my behalf,
a messenger from a remembering man;
take your way from your bunk at Menai
unswervingly to Lisbon;
swim along there awhile
to the edge of Spain, heart of the world.
You are a heavenly swimmer,
swim to the chase, you lively one.
Ask at the water's limit
(let us give praise!) for a soldier,
Pirs Gruffudd, who saddened all breasts,
pearl of true faith, pure heart,
the honour of Penrhyn, its fine son,
gentle lord, lustiest of men.
It is six weary years
since he took ship abroad,
to the seas beyond the estuary,
over the bar across the world.
It's time for the gallant giver
to turn away from salt water
and come, ending anxiety,
to his own hall from that foul place,
to stay where I like to see him
and to please his people in this.
When, after this effort, you see him,
courageous upon his ship
in gleaming harness, call to him
a message on my behalf,
address him profitably
in copious verse from a companion
lovingly, from a man who once
sailed on the same journey
until, agreeable confession,
he bought knowledge as things went ill.
Then truly he forswore
the sea and all its ventures.
Now give a grunt and tell him,
beseech him to evade this fate
and soon to leave the sea

to others from now on.
There's little profit to be gained
waiting at dusk on the cold waters,
and much shame and evil comes
easily from sea-faring to-day.
It's good for a brisk man to leave the shore,
to sail the sea far over the world
to gain, in spite of the constraining cold
true knowledge of this world.
But it's not good or godly
to keep on in this way.
Show his kin's unsatisfied hearts,
the fruit of a bitter cause.
When the wind blows and things look bad,
a high wind comes over the hillside,
the world goes mad and ugly,
there's praying and loud wailing
lest the wind, in this deep danger,
endanger his grey-headed body.
Many are then to be seen
groaning for his coming to land,
unable to sleep, in heart-break
and dreams; I've heard it much spoken of.
Wasters now go sea-faring,
men who own not a foot of land.
Let him be tamed to returning
from their company to ours.
Let him come home, devotedly
to lead his men to his fine land,
Captain of the azure *Grace*
and a clean-handed captain.
May God in his grace grant him as a gift
the grace to quit the sea.

46. *A Welsh Ballad*

upon the measure *About the Bank of Helicon*

A shout came from the loquacious ones
whom we heard yesterday under green trees,
    holy and church-like place,
three lives to those gentle poets,
grove linnet, innocent nightingale,
    pensive and paradisal,
sweet thrush of pure oration,
the blackbird greater in desire
and the lascivious siskin
who net the song of the lark,
    singing,
    plucking
    so much poetry,
    so lively,
    so clearly,
and in their true lusting.

A near-by grove with notes increasing,
an April grove and primrose-full,
    place of fine song and daisies;
a dale full of the spring clover
and the green clothes of true delight
    filling with happiness,
with flowers on the thorn points,
the slim birch and the fresh leaves;
fair is the fountain, sweet the spot,
from under boughs there springs
    the clear water,
    the fresh water;
    fair, fortunate place,
    a place to sleep,
    a place to learn
all knots of descanting.

I'd have all sweetness in my house,
both the song of Gwynedd's darling
     to some sprightly music
and an Irish girl called Eurwedd,
unyoked pair of laughing girls
     in shining green tree mansion,
to sing loud of happy summers
all with bird song entwined;
profitably to sing to God
a golden cycle of great praise;
     a tuning up
     of psalmody
     in varying notes;
     devices,
     turning voices
  for unnumbered ages.

Many tree-clusters, open woodlands,
many a column deeply fashioned,
     many a clear knot of praise;
a peaceful place full of sweet chords
of the plentiful praise that's made
     by the meadow-dwellers;
each bird in its own voice,
each tree in bright green tunic,
each plant in its own virtue,
each bird with a poet's lips,
     not suffering
     but sprightly
     in heavenly notes;
     not troubled
     but in treble;
  the place is Venus's.

Delight is good for all mankind
and merriment for maidens,
     Sunday is good for men;
this is fair and not odious for age,
fair, not unpleasant, for youth.

Sunday is good for men,
planned fair by the true God Father,
his gift and notable grace.
Each voice is fair, every turn,
as long as there's no sin.
    On earth
    how gentle;
    early on the wheat
    and on the grove;
    how mild the land
where the great blessing's given!

47. The Lover's Shirt

As I was washing under a span
of the bridge of Cardigan
and in my hand my lover's shirt
with a golden beetle to drub the dirt,
a man came to me on a steed,
broad in shoulder, proud in speed,
and he asked me if I'd sell
the shirt of the lad I love so well.

But I said I wouldn't sell
for a hundred pounds and packs as well,
nor if the grass of two ridges were deep
in wethers and the whitest sheep,
nor if two hay meadows were choked
with oxen which were ready yoked,
nor if St. David's nave were filled
with herbs all pressed but not distilled.
Not even for all that would I sell
the shirt of the lad I love so well.

Notes

1. Gododdin was the name of a tribe of North Britain living in what is to-day South East Scotland. Ptolemy the Geographer refers to them as Otadenoi. The name of the tribe was given to its heroic poem, *Gododdin*. Catraeth, as Sir Ifor Williams has shown, is the Catarracta or Cataractonium of the Romans, the Catterick of the English. Mynyddog Mwynfawr ruled from Dineiddyn or Dunedin. It is to be remembered that the Britons used horses in battle even before the Romans came and that they had learnt much about armour and fighting from the Romans. The English had neither horses nor such equipment. The odds of 300 trained commandos against thousands of the enemy are not incredible. Sir Ifor Williams dates this battle between 580-600, and this was when Aneirin lived and sang in Edinburgh.

    Mr. David Jones used the last line but one of the Issac stanza as the motto to his *In Parenthesis*, where this battle is related to the 1914-18 War.

2. Taliesin was another late sixth-century poet of North Britain, this time of Rheged, to-day the counties of Kirkcudbright, Wigtown and part of Ayr. He wrote in praise of Urien, King of Rheged, and his son Owain, both of whom fought against the Angles under Hussa, son of Ida. Hussa may be the Fflamddwyn or Flame-bearer of this poem.

    The text used for this translation was that of the *Book of Taliesin*, a manuscript of *c.* 1275.

3. Sir Ifor Williams has shown Heledd and Llywarch Hen to be not poets of the sixth or early seventh century but central figures in saga cycles composed in the ninth century. Pengwern is the modern Shrewsbury. Heledd, daughter of Cyndrwyn, here laments the death of her brother, Cynddylan, and the destruction of their home by the Mercians.

    The text used is that of *CLlH*.

4. Llywarch, in spite of doubts about him as a poet, was a historical person, a prince of North Britain during the sixth century. Hence the connection here with Urien Rheged.

    The text used is that of *CLlH*.

5. As Sir Ifor Williams says, only a similarity of style and the resulting accident of scribal assembling link this poem with Llywarch Hen and his saga. The sick man may have been a leper. I have here abstracted

the cuckoo sequence, the first ten *englynion* or thirty lines, from this poem.

The text used is that of *CLlH*.

6.   The names of some of these ancient British heroes are familiar to English readers in other forms. Cynfelyn is Cymbeline and his son Coel may be King Cole. Beli, the last of the heroes in the sequence, takes us back beyond history and legend to the Celtic gods. His name is remembered in Billingsgate.

Sir Ifor Williams believes this to be a collection of tail pieces originally belonging to the stories of the life and death of the people concerned. If this is so the stanzas have been not unskilfully strung together in *BBC* with an introductory opening and suitable conclusion, and with suitable questions occasionally to hold the interest. The sequence thus forms a complete poem, and one can imagine the poet or the narrator pausing, like a good entertainer, to ask his hearers in the hall for requests.

> Whose is this grave?
> It's so and so's grave;
> ask me, I know.

> *Piau y bedd hwn?*
> *Bedd hwn a hwn:*
> *gofyn i mi, mi a'i gwn.*

There are 72 of these fascinating stanzas in *BBC*, but no edited text of them has ever been published. I have translated others in *IWP*.

The text used here is that of *BBC*.

7.   This is the earliest and grimmest view we have of the Gereint of romance. Llongborth must have been a harbour in Southern England.

The text used is that of *BBC*.

8.   Meilyr Brydydd, or Meilyr the Poet, who lived during the early part of the twelfth century, was chief poet to Gruffudd ap Cynan, King of Gwynedd. Meilyr's son, Gwalchmai, and his grandsons were also poets. *Marwysgafn* meant deathbed, *ysgafn* being derived from the Latin *scamnum* (bench). Cynddelw and Bleddyn Fardd also wrote poems with the same title. Enlli is Bardsey in English.

9.   Cynddelw Brydydd Mawr, or Cynddelw the Great Poet, who wrote during the second half of the twelfth century, was perhaps

the greatest master of his craft in that century. He wrote in praise of princes of North and South Wales.

The text used here is that of *PG*.

10. Gwalchmai, son of Meilyr, flourished during the middle of the twelfth century, and sang in praise of Owain Gwynedd. His blending of the themes of love, nature and war is similar to that effected by Hywel ab Owain, whom he must have known well, but it is not known which of the two poets first ventured upon this departure from the conventions of bardism. Like Hywel, Gwalchmai described the Battle of Tal y Moelfre and was probably present at it, for Gwalchmai was a warrior as well as a poet. A landowner too, as the place name Trewalchmai indicates.

The text used is that of *H*. 32 lines have been omitted where lacunae make the text obscure. *V*. H., pp. 18–20.

11–18. Hywel ab Owain Gwynedd was the son of the great Owain, King of Gwynedd, and an Irish girl called Pyfog. He died in 1170 after a life of internecine and anti-Norman warfare. All his extant verse is translated here. The original is in the *Hendregadredd MS*.

Caer Lliwelydd is the modern Carlisle; Kerry is in Montgomeryshire; Maelienydd is a region of Central Wales; Rheged is South Western Scotland; Tegeingl is the North Eastern corner of Wales.

Garwy Hir is one of the legendary great lovers of Britain. Ogrfan is variously said to have been king of the underworld, father of Guinevere and father of Ceridwen, who may have been a fertility goddess and muse of poetry. Cynddelw, in his lament for the death of Rhirid Flaidd, associates Ogrfan and Ceridwen. See Sir John Rhys, *Celtic Heathendom*, pp. 267–9, for Ogrfan's cauldron and his connection with the alphabet. For the form Gogfran see p. 65. The battle described is that of Tal y Moelfre, at which Hywel fought at his father's side against Henry II's army and fleet, the latter reinforced by foreign contingents. Gwalchmai also describes this battle.

19. Gruffudd ab yr Ynad Coch belongs to the second half of the thirteenth century. This great poem is the only one attributed to him with certainty. Llywelyn ap Gruffudd was the last independent ruler of Wales and this poem expresses a suitable and unusual feeling of awful tragedy and national disaster. It is something of a *tour de force* in that it has only one main end rhyme throughout its considerable length.

The translator is faced with difficulties such as the ambiguity in the use of the word *penn* which cannot be rendered by one word in English. *Penn milwr*, for instance, means both a soldier's head and a soldier-leader. Llywelyn's head was displayed on a stake for the mockery of Londoners. See Gwynfor Evans, *Aros Mae*, plate facing p. 176. The text used is that of *PRBH*.

20.   Gruffudd ab Adda was a poet and a musician as well as the author of two famous essays in poetic prose (see *Yr Areithiau Pros*, D. Gwenallt Jones. Welsh Univ. Press 1934). He was a contemporary of Dafydd ap Gwilym, who lamented his death in verse. The pacification of Welsh life in the fourteenth century is well reflected in this poem, but Gruffudd ab Adda himself died in a friendly scuffle.

The text used is that of *CDGG*.

21–23.   The dates of Dafydd ap Gwilym's life are not known, but he flourished during the middle decades of the fourteenth century. He was born at Llanbadarn in Cardiganshire and was buried at Strata Florida Abbey. The idea has now been abandoned that Morfudd and Dyddgu were just any fair or dark-haired girl respectively, with whom Dafydd was for the moment in love, and Dr. Thomas Parry has established the case for their having been real women. Dafydd wrote about thirty poems to Morfudd, and the poems show her to have been blonde, of noble birth, married, a native of Northern Cardiganshire and not unwilling to continue to receive the poet to the arms he celebrated in a *cywydd*. Of Morfudd's husband Dafydd made the type of a jealous cuckold, who became a stock character in poetry for more than two hundred years after.

In *The Woodland Mass* Dafydd employs the wandering scholar's trick of using religious terminology to speak of nature and love-making, but it is possible to recognise an awareness of the ubiquity of the glory of God here rather than blasphemy.

The Rattle Bag is a fine example of the vituperative, rabelaisian mode much affected by fourteenth-century poets, especially Dafydd's often unprintable contemporaries Madog Dwygraig and Dafydd y Coed. The heaping together of compound descriptive words, such as we see in the line: *greithgrest garegddwyn grothgro*, was one of the skills of the mediaeval Welsh craftsman in words, and Dafydd was our greatest master of it.

The text used here is that of *GDG*.

24. Llywelyn Goch ap Meurig Hen wrote during the second half of the fourteenth century. Most of his verse is in the traditional range of praise to patrons in the *awdl* form, but in this *cywydd* he does something staggeringly new in singing an aubade to a dead girl, who sleeps too long in her dark earth-bed.

The text used is that of *CDGG*.

25-6. Iolo Goch, a master poet of wide learning and scope in subject matter, flourished during the second half of the fourteenth century. He wrote in praise of Owain Glyndŵr and his hall at Sycharth. No one appreciated comfort, food and drink, and the respect due to a master poet more than Iolo, or expressed this better in verse.

Hu Gadarn, or Hugh the Strong, is the Hugue li Forz of the twelfth century French metrical *Pélerinage de Charlemagne*, which was translated into Welsh in the fourteenth century. A Welsh text is included in the *Red Book of Hergest* and this was translated into English by Sir John Rhys for Koschwitz's treatise on the French poem (*Heilbronn* 1879). The description of a fourteenth-century plough is detailed and exact.

The text used is that of *CIGE*.

27. Siôn Cent (Anglicé John Kent, for Siôn is pronounced Shone) wrote during the early decades of the fifteenth century. It is not easy to distinguish his identity, except as a poet, from that of other John Kents, John Kemps and John a Kents of the fifteenth century. He recommended the remembrance of death to the proud and wealthy ones of this world and was the first poet to be consistently unflattering in his reference to the landed aristocracy.

The sectional form of this *cywydd*, with its refrain, is unusual in Welsh.

The text used is that of *CIGE*.

28-31. Dafydd ab Edmwnd, who flourished during the second half of the fifteenth century, was a poet of love and nature in the tradition of Dafydd ap Gwilym. A great craftsman in verse, he was responsible for the tightening up of the twenty-four strict measures of versification at the Carmarthen Eisteddfod of 1451. Living at a time when many poets were involved in the Wars of the Roses, Dafydd ab Edmwnd avoided politics, but his attitude towards England is made clear in his lament for his dead friend Siôn Eos, the harpist.

In the poem concealing the identity of his love it is interesting to see Welsh forms of Norman-French girls' names Sioned, Annes, Alswn, Alis and Isabel take their place alongside the accustomed Gwenhwyfar, Gwenllian and Nest.

Siôn Eos would be John Nightingale in English.

The text used for the Dafydd ab Edmwnd translations is based on *GDE*, except that of the poem *I Wallt Merch*, which is from *YFN*.

32. Bedo Aeddren or Aurdrem flourished about the year 1500. His work is confused in the manuscripts with that of Bedo Brwynlys and some of his verse, including this poem, has been attributed to Dafydd ap Gwilym. This Easter poem is clearly in the Dafydd ap Gwilym tradition and has rare freshness and light. It was printed as Dafydd's work in *BDG* but is rejected by Sir Ifor Williams and Dr. Thomas Parry.

The text here used is that of *MS Llanstephan* 133 *p.* 1066.

33. Lewis Glyn Cothi took his name from the Cothi valley in Northern Carmarthenshire, where he was born. He took the Lancastrian side in the Wars of the Roses and got into trouble for it. He lived during the middle and second half of the fifteenth century.

Saint Dwynwen was the daughter of the fifth-century Brychan Brycheiniog and the patroness of lovers.

Lewis Glyn Cothi's work has been edited by Mr. E. D. Jones since this translation was made. The text here used is based on the early sixteenth century *MS Llanstephan* 7, where the poem is headed 'Marwnat John y Glynn mab v mlwydd Lewis y Glynn i Dat ai Kant', 'Lament for the death of John of the Valley, five years old son of Lewis of the Valley, sung by his father'.

34. Tudur Aled, a native of Llansannan in Denbighshire, flourished 1480–1526. Like Dafydd ap Gwilym and Dafydd ab Edmwnd, he was of noble stock. He was a strict upholder of tradition in poetry and an appreciater of good fare. No Welsh poet has written in more lively fashion or with keener observation of animals. The poem of asking became a conventional type, affording the poet the opportunity to exercise his ingenuity in the invention of comparisons.

The text used here is that of *YFN*.

35–6. The text of these *englynion* is based on that of *MS Mostyn* 131, (pp. 132 and 440), a collection of *englynion* by many authors in the hand of John Jones, Gelli Lyfdy, written between 1605 and 1618.

37.   This is a selection from an *englyn* sequence of considerable charm. T. Gwynn Jones copied some of them for his *Gelfyddyd Gwta*, printed them as separate *englynion* and altered them.

The text used is based on that of *MS Mostyn* 131 (p. 9).

38.   It was William Thomas's chaplain, Syr Siôn Gruffudd, who wrote the well-known *Hiraeth am Gaernarfon*, when they were together in Flanders *c.* 1586.

The text used is based on that of *MS Mostyn* 131 (p. 311).

39.   Robin Clidro, a native of the Clwyd valley, was a wandering poet of the *clerwr* or lower class who lived during the second half of the sixteenth century. An elegy by Siôn Tudur tells us that he was killed by a highwayman in South Wales. His poetry is lively and amusing and he used verse form and *cynghanedd* with a cheerfully unbardic freedom for which one is thankful.

The text used here is that of *MS Cwrt Mawr* 24, a manuscript of the seventeenth century. An incomplete copy of this poem was printed by T. Gwynn Jones in his *Llên Cymru* Vol. III.

40.   The Cynon River is a tributary of the Taff. The text used is that of *CRhC*.

Rowenna, daughter of Hengist, was given the name Alis Ronwen in a Triad. The English kings decended from her marriage with Vortigern were called Alice's children by the Welsh.

41.   This is the second scene of the five-act tragedy. In the main the unknown author depends on Chaucer and Henryson, selecting freely and translating closely from them. But there is no known source for this version of Cressida's trial, which may therefore be taken to be original writing. The author was a scholar who found no difficulty in reading Chaucer and Henryson. He must have formed his notion of dramatic structure and tragic irony in the Elizabethan London theatre. His tragedy, though not as great or as original as Shakespeare's *Troilus and Cressida*, gives an entirely different presentation of the story and has more unity.

Mr. Herbert Davies's production of my prepared text of *Troelus a Chresyd* at the Ystradgynlais National Eisteddfod of 1954 (the first known performance) showed that this unique Welsh tragedy can hold the theatre.

The text used is that of *MS Peniarth* 106, the sole version, which was written by John Jones, Gelli Lyfdy. About half of it was completed by February 1613 and the rest by the autumn of 1622. It is clearly a copy. The play must have been written *c*. 1600.

42. William Cynwal wrote this poem to defend women against the attack upon them written in a Skeltonic metre by an unknown poet earlier in the sixteenth century, a poem which I translated in *The Rent that's Due to Love*, Poetry London, 1950 and more fully in *Against Women*, Golden Cockerel Press, 1953. Cynwal, who died in 1587 or 1588, took one of his poetic grades at the Caerwys Eisteddfod of 1568. He was a strict observer of the bardic traditions, but here he descends to a stanza form of the free metres, such as an unqualified poet of the lowest order might have used, since the subject matter of this poem is outside the conventional range of the master poet.

The text used is that of *CRhC*.

43–5. Thomas Prys, of Plas Iolyn, Denbighshire, was a landowner, a soldier, a pirate and a good poet. The dates of his life are *c*. 1564–1634. He was at Tilbury with the Queen in 1588 and fought in the Low Countries, probably with Sir Roger Williams. He knew London well, its great houses, taverns, brothels and prisons, and has some amusing and some bitter things to say about it. More than 200 of his *cywyddau* have come down to us and they are all worth reading. No poet in Welsh has as wide a scope of subject or writes in a more lively way. Nor was he deficient in the traditional skill of versification in the strict metres.

The text used for this translation is that of *MS Mostyn* 112, which may be in the poet's hand, with occasional readings from the Cefn Coch MSS. Many of the phrases are in English, with a Welsh spelling. I have anglicised the spelling of these phrases and italicised them here.

A note in the margin of this manuscript informs us that *Grace* was the name of Pirs Gruffudd's ship. Pirs, to whom Prys sends the porpoise as a messenger, was Prys's cousin and heir to the Penrhyn estate, but he was not wise enough to give up buccaneering, as Prys did, and he got into more and more trouble. Pirs Gruffudd died in 1628 and was buried in Westminster Abbey.

46. Edmwnd Prys, Archdeacon of Merioneth, lived from 1544–1623. He helped in the translation of the Bible into Welsh and versified the Psalms. He wrote both in the free and strict metres. He carried on a long controversy in verse with William Cynwal, who considered him

no poet at all, so prepared was he to use popular and even foreign stanza forms, as in this Welsh Ballad.

The text used is from *CRhC*.

47.   The text of this song is from *CRhC*.

Abbreviations

BBC: *The Black Book of Carmarthen:* Reproduced by J. G. Evans, Pwllheli, 1907.

BDG: *Barddoniaeth Dafydd ap Gwilym:* William Owen and Owen Jones, London, 1789.

CA: *Canu Aneirin:* Ifor Williams, Cardiff, 1938.

CDGG: *Cywyddau Dafydd ap Gwilym a'i Gyfoeswyr:* T. Roberts and Ifor Williams, Bangor, 1914. (2nd ed. Cardiff, 1935.)

CIGE: *Cywyddau Iolo Goch ac Eraill:* Henry Lewis, Thomas Roberts and Ifor Williams, Cardiff, 1937.

CLlH: *Canu Llywarch Hen:* Ifor Williams, Cardiff, 1935.

CRhC: *Canu Rhydd Cynnar:* T. H. Parry-Williams, Cardiff, 1932.

GDE: *Gwaith Dafydd ab Edmwnd:* T. Roberts, Bangor, 1914.

GDG: *Gwaith Dafydd ap Gwilym:* T. Parry, Cardiff, 1952.

H: *The Hendregadredd Manuscript:* Rh. Morris Jones, J. Morris Jones and T. H. Parry-Williams, Cardiff, 1953.

IWP: *An Introduction to Welsh Poetry:* Gwyn Williams, London, 1953.

PG: *The Poetry of the Gogynfeirdd:* E. Anwyl, Denbigh, 1909.

PRBH: *Poetry from the Red Book of Hergest:* J. G. Evans, Pwllheli, 1911.

YFN: *Y Flodeugerdd Newydd:* W. J. Gruffydd, Cardiff, 1909.

Index

Abercuawg, 10, 23
Aberffraw, 34, 46
Aeddan, 19
Aeron, 17
Aneirin, 10, 11, 17
Antenor, 92
Araith Ddychan i'r Gwragedd, 14
Argoed Llwyfain, 20
Arnold, Matthew, 9
Arthur, 27, 59, 65
Auden, W. H., 9

Bedo Aeddren, 13, 76, 121
Beidog, 25
Beli, son of Benlli, 26, 117
Brigid, Saint, 101
Burlings, The, 106

Caerwys, 32
Caerwys Eisteddfod, 123
Calcas, 91, 93
Caradawg, 18
Caradoc, 99
Cardigan (Aberteifi), 115
Carmarthen (Caerfyrddin), 33, 120
Catherine, Saint, 98
Catlew, 17
Catraeth, 17–9, 116
Catterick, 10, 116
Ceredig, 18
Ceres, 101
Ceridwen, 118, 122
chaplet of Iseult, 79
Charlemagne, 65, 120
Chirk (Y Waun), 74
Clidro, Robin, 87, 122
Coed Glyn Cynon, 14

Coed Marchan, 14
Coel, son of Cynfelyn, 20, 25, 117
Coleridge, 9
Cressid, 108
Cresyd, 91–5
Cricieth, 63
Cynddelw, 10, 11, 31, 117
Cynddylan, 21, 116
Cynfarch, 22
Cynfelyn (Cymbeline), 25, 117
Cynon, 17
Cynvan, 19
Cynwal, William, 14, 96, 123

Dafydd ab Edmwnd, 13, 16, 68, 120
Dafydd ap Gwilym, 9, 12, 13, 50, 119–121
Dafydd Nanmor, 13
Dafydd y Coed, 119
David, King, 66, 100

Dumbarton, 35
Dwynwen, Saint, 78, 121
Dyfwy, 20

Edward III, 13
Edwin, 33
Elias, 101
Elucidarium (Lusudarus), 60
Eneas, 92
Enlli, 30
Erbin, 63
Esther, 101

Fflamddwyn, 20, 116
Finn Fragment, 10

Garwy Hir, 52
Generys, 38
Genilles, 32
Gereint, 27, 117
Glyn Cynon Wood, 89–90
Goddau, 20
Gododdin, 10–1, 17, 116
Gruffudd ab Adda, 12, 49, 119
Gruffudd ab yr Ynad Coch, 11,
    46, 118
Gruffudd, Pirs, 110, 123
Gruffudd, Syr Siôn, 122
Guinevere (Gwenhwyfar), 65, 72,
    118
Gwalchmai, 10, 32, 117
Gwawrddur, 19
Gweirfyl, 37
Gwên ap Llywarch Hen, 25
Gwenfrewi, 99
Gwenllian, 37
Gwgawn, 19, 76
Gwiawn, 19
Gwladus, 37
Gwriad, 18
Gwrien, 18
Gwyddneu, 18
Gwyn, 18–9

Hawis, 38
Hector, 93–5
Helen of Troy, 108
Helena, 98
Helenus, 91, 93
Helicon, About the Bank of, 112
Henryson, 122
Holland, Hugh, 14
Hu Gadarn, 60, 120
Hunydd, 38

Hussa, 116
Hywel ab Owain Gwynedd, 10–1,
    36, 118
Hywel Dda, 13, 74
Hywel of the Axe, Sir, 12, 62

Ieuan, 18
Indeg, 57
Iolo Goch, 12–3, 59, 120
Isis, 102
Issac, 18, 116

Jehosaba, 100
Jonas, 100
Jonathan, 100
Jones, David (*In Parenthesis, The
    Anathemata, Merlin Land*), 11,
    116
Jones, John, Gelli Lyfdy, 121–2
Jones, T. Gwynn, 122
Julius Caesar, 16

Keats, 9

Lazarus, 100
Lewis Glyn Cothi, 13, 78, 121
Lisbon, 110
Llanbadarn, 52, 119
Lleucu, 37
Lleucu Llwyd, 13, 56
Llongborth, 27, 117
Llywarch Hen, 116
Llywelyn ap Gruffudd, 46, 118
Llywelyn Goch, 13, 56, 119
Llywelyn, son of Madoc, 31

Mabinogion, 9
Madawg, 18
Madog Dwygraig, 119

Maelgwn, 35
Maes Garnedd, 35
Marchan Wood, 87
Marchlew, 17–8
Margaret, Saint, 99
Martha, 100
Mary Magdalen, 98
Meilyr, 11, 29, 117
Merlin, 37
Milky Way, The, 70
Morfudd, 50, 72, 119
Mynyddawg Mwynfawr, 10, 17
Myrddin, 10

Nest, 38
Nicostrata, 101

Ogrfan (Ogyrvann), 43, 118
Owain ap Eulad, 18
Owain ap Urien, 20, 22, 25
Owain Cyfeiliog, 10, 65
Owain Glyndŵr, 13, 120
Owain Gwynedd, 32–5, 118

Paris, 92
Parry, Dr. Thomas, 119, 121
Pengwern, 21, 116
Peredur, 19
Priaf, King of Troy, 91–2, 95
Pryderi, 25
Prys, Edmwnd, 112, 123
Prys, Thomas, 13–5, 105, 123
Ptolemy the Geographer, 116
Pyll, 18

Quinze Joyes de Mariage, Les, 14

Rachel, 100
Rebecca, 100

Rheged, 20, 37, 118
Rhuddlan, 33
Rhufawn Hir, 19
Rhufawn Pebyr, 36
Rhydderch Hael, 25
Rhys, Sir John, 118, 120

St. David's, 115
Schole House of Women, The, 14
Scilly, 106
Seafarer, 9
Shakespeare, Coriolanus, 14, Troilus and Cressida, 122
Sinon, 91, 95
Siôn Cent, 13, 65, 120
Siôn Eos, 13, 74, 120
Siôn y Glyn, 78, 121
Solomon (Selyf), 66
Spenser, Edmund, 9, 14
Sibyls, The, 102

Taliesin, 10, 20, 116
Tal y Moelfre, 118
Tegwedd (Tegfedd), 65
Teirtu (Teirtud), 75
Thomas, Dylan, 9, 11, 12
Thomas, William, 86, 122
Troelus, 93–5
Troelus a Chresyd, 14, 122
Tudur Aled, 13, 80, 121
Tudor, Henry, 13

Uriad, 25
Urien, 25
Urien Rheged, 12, 20, 22, 116

Virgil (Fferyll), 66

Williams, Sir Ifor, 116–7, 121